The A
Awakening the Soul

Practical Yoga-Mysticism

Prashant S. Shah

Amazon.com, Amazon.in and Kindle e-books

© **Copyright, February 2011;**
revised Nov 2015; Second Edition Sept 2018
by Prashant Shivanand Shah

ISBN-13: 978-1460906033
ISBN-10: 1460906039
ASIN: B00AX19BRW

Address: H-901 Nilamber Bellissimo, Vasna-Bhayli Road, Vadodara 391 410, Gujarat, India.
Email: prashantshah@alum.mit.edu
Site on Internet at http://spiritual-living.in

Note:

All rights reserved, including the right to reproduce this book or portions of it in any form whatsoever. However, permission is granted to make brief excerpts in quotation marks concluded with the note: "From **The Art of Awakening the Soul** by Prashant S. Shah; http://spiritual-living.in"

The Contents

Abstract 8

Foreword 9

What our Readers Write 13

Introduction 16

What is Mysticism? 22

The Practice 29

The Basic Task 34

The Inner Work 42

The practical side of purification 50

a) Purifying the mind from thoughts 50

b) Purifying the mind from emotions 51

c) Purification in the body 53

d) On correcting your mistakes 54

Transformation 56

The Message 68

© 2011-2018, Prashant S. Shah

Aphorisms 71

1. Call the presence of God 72

2. Extend the spiritual feeling into your everyday life 74

3. Involve God in your life 76

4. Follow God 78

5. The attitude with which you do your work always matters 80

6. Do not lower yourself in the eyes of your conscience 82

7. Your enemies are within you 84

8. Do not impose your way on God 86

9. God always supports disinterested action 88

A Prayer 90

An Assurance: 91

A Conversation 93

Conversation continued: 95
Conclusion: 96

Moments of Overflowing 98

© 2011-2018, Prashant S. Shah

1. The Call 99
2. Patient Waiting 100
3. The Ego 102
4. Your Cupbearer 103
5. You Lead and I Follow 104
6. You Are My Strength 106
7. I Live For You 107
8. The Awakening 109

A Journey into the Higher Worlds 110

1. Our condition at the beginning 111
2. Taking control of our attention 112
3. The nature of the subconscious 113
4. What we see in the subconscious 114
5. The inner battle 115
6. After the victory 117
7. The separate awareness 118
8. The purpose of the separate awareness 119
9. Awareness beyond the mind 120

Spiritual Alchemy 122

1. The world as consciousness 123

2. Our personal consciousness 124

3. The human situation 125

4. What is Bondage? 126

5. The Separation 126

6. What is Purification? 127

7. The Alchemical Marriage 128

The Coming of the New Era 130

The two levels of our consciousness 131

The Process of Spiritual Growth 134

The Spiritual Purpose of our life 135

The Coming of the New Era 137

How can I Participate? 141

On Promoting a Spiritual Mission 143

A Review Request 145

Appendix 146

About the Author 146

© 2011-2018, Prashant S. Shah

About Darshana Centre 149

Books 156

1. Healing Without Drugs 156

2. Solving the Problems of Life...........160

3. The Biochemic Prescriber..............162
   The Contents 164

4. How to Restore your Health Naturally..........166
   Contents 167

© 2011-2018, Prashant S. Shah

ABSTRACT

Mysticism is the pursuit of God. But God has a presence in the Soul. Hence, by meditating on God you bring the Soul forward in your life.

The Soul is the true purpose of your life on earth. So, when it awakens everything in your life begins to find its proper place: You know what you have come to do; and you get the opportunities that you really need.

The Soul will thrill you with its love and beauty. It will give you the deep experience of love and fulfilment that cannot be got from people or things of the world.

The experience of the Soul brings with it newer faculties. Then you are no longer limited to the intellectual process of inferring and figuring things out. You can look into the mind of things and know everything intuitively.

© 2011-2018, Prashant S. Shah

Foreword

By the Author

There comes a stage in our life when we feel that there is more to living than just satisfying the desires of the body and ambitions of the mind. We want to know the deeper meaning and purpose of our existence on earth.

As our involvement in the search deepens we arrive at a stage where no amount of indirect inferences or explanations can satisfy us. We cannot feel fulfilled unless we enter into direct communication with the spiritual presence that mysteriously underlies our existence.

This is the mystical quest and this book shows you how to pursue it.

The book narrates the practical side of spiritual growth in the way of yoga-mysticism. It explores the psychological processes that go along with this growth, and the esoteric practices that are used by the oriental mystics to mature our spiritual awareness and transform our personal nature.

People often ask: *"What exactly is mysticism?"* Here we explain it as an art of awakening the soul and bringing it forward in our life.

The soul carries a God Presence in it. Hence, the basic practice of mysticism is to attune the mind with God consciousness. Then, instead of leading a life that is guided by the desires and tendencies of our mind and body, we are guided by the promptings of a higher consciousness.

About the book

This book started out as an article. I wrote it for the students of my correspondence course on Yoga-Mysticism. The article was well received, and hence in 2009 I brought out a small booklet edition of it titled *'The Practice of Mysticism'*. For the booklet edition I added a few aphorisms, a prayer, and a conversation.

Then, in October 2010, I was invited to conduct a workshop in New York based on this booklet. In the workshop we discussed each passage of the booklet in great detail. It gave me the opportunity to expand on the ideas and provide deeper insights.

© 2011-2018, Prashant S. Shah

These ideas and insights are given as *'insightful notes'* in this book. They make the subject very interesting and much easier to grasp. These notes have been revised in this second edition.

After the workshop we had many interesting discussions on the 'Art of Awakening'. Many of the participants suggested that I should include some of my earlier writings on the subject in this book. Accordingly I added some articles. They will give you a many sided view of the mystic pursuit. The articles are:

Moments of Overflowing.
A Journey into the Higher Worlds.
Spiritual Alchemy; and
The Coming of the New Era.

A brief description of the articles is as follows:
'Moments of Overflowing' consists of eight poems. They illustrate the actual stages in the awakening that arise on the path of mysticism.
'A Journey into the Higher Worlds' explains the journey into the 'cosmos within'. It talks of the phantoms you encounter on the way and how to make the journey safe.
'Spiritual Alchemy' is a rare insight into the process

of transforming your nature. Alchemy speaks of transforming lead into gold. In the spiritual context it is the process of shifting your identity from being a narrow and inferring mind, to being a wider soul-consciousness.

'The Coming of the New Era' characterises the present cosmic situation with a view to show how the practice of mysticism can help you in facing it. It is followed by an outline of the correspondence *courses of Darshana Centre*. They provide you with the opportunity to follow up the study with practice.

I am very grateful to Madanda G. Machayya for organising the workshops in New York and for encouraging me to write this book. I am grateful to all the course participants for their questions, insights and suggestions. I must thank the readers for contributing their reviews.

Prashant S. Shah

© 2011-2018, Prashant S. Shah

WHAT OUR READERS WRITE

1.   This book is really great. It puts me into a Trance! I feel it is directly speaking to me and quietly leading me into some great mystery. Wow! The *'insightful notes'* are superb and far out of this world. The book is a 'must read' for anyone doing serious spiritual practice. *Ginger M* (Through Amazon.com)

2.   A great book on the spiritual journey written in very simple language: There are lots of books out there, but this is the first one I came across that gave so many details of spiritual journey in a simple language, along with some techniques... After every important paragraph there are 'Insightful Notes' that are a great help to understand and appreciate the deeper meaning. The overall clarity of the content has increased as a result.

What I like most in this book is that it speaks directly and is to the point. It is also logically very sound. Of course, one needs to read it more than once to digest the content. This book certainly has the strength to trigger of some deep thinking. By *Yong (Zen Master)* (Reviewed on Amazon.com)

3. Just 2 weeks back I received a copy of this book from Amazon and I have been using it ever since. It has summarized everything that I learnt in the spiritual workshops over the past 11 years; and it has much more! The format is very simple to follow and the insights are out of this world.

The book now sits on my altar. I use it before my daily meditation. I read just one chapter at a time. Then I go over it again and again to become more aware of what I really need to do. I plan to continue this as a part of an ongoing process. It really helps a lot to have a simple and easy-to-follow guide like this book. I can open it at any time and look up the part that is relevant or reminds me of what I need to do. I thank you for writing up the book in the way you did. It is a spiritual gem. *Ludy R*, ludy_mr@hotmail.com

4. I have read this book a number of times. It feels as much compressed as the proverbial diamond. Again, it also speaks directly to my day-to-day life. It has helped me put myself into God's hands. I don't think any book can do more.

The Art Of Awakening The Soul Pg. 15

Professor Frank Sanchez, Ph.D. New York,
Nyudonne@aol.com

5.	Excellent. The subtle changes that occur on spiritual path are explained with great clarity. You can really relate to it and know exactly where you need to make improvements. (Reviewed on 24-1-2013 in Amazon.com) *Saket Vaidya,* vaidya_saket@yahoo.com

6.	This book is more like the direct personal experience of the author. It explains the spiritual journey in simple language, but in a very striking way that really touches the heart. *Sanjeev V,* sanjeev1657@gmail

7.	I've just finished reading your new manuscript. The chapters 'Transformation' and 'The Message' are wonderful... The idea of coming close to God or to people who have walked with God has always fascinated me; and science is not going to rob me of this fascination... I'm often asked: *"What is Yoga-Mysticism?"* This is how I explain it: Yoga without God is Patanjali Yoga; yoga with God is Shiva Yoga; and Yoga-Mysticism is how you describe it to the American readers. *M.J.G.*

© 2011-2018, Prashant S. Shah

INTRODUCTION

By Madanda G. Machayya

In mid-1974, I had just finished my MBA studies and started my working career in Bombay (present-day Mumbai). In order to broaden my perspective of life, I participate in some self-development courses that were being hosted by the Indo-American Chamber of Commerce. That is where I first met the author. He had freshly returned from USA after finishing his studies there. I was among the first of his students to sign up for his course on **"Natural, Mystic and Occult Philosophy"**. I had read some metaphysical writings, but no one had explained this subject so clearly to me before. It was a major turning point in my life. Something changed inside me, and I felt committed to doing serious spiritual practice.

During the next few years I actively sought the author's company to absorb and understand as much of his thought process as possible. His was one of the most remarkable minds that I had ever met. He showed a deep understanding and insight into many subjects, esoteric and secular, and had a wide range of world views. In India, spiritual subjects are taught in a manner that is not easily accessible to someone who is trained and educated in the modern way. Hence, it was very inspiring to find someone who could cross this barrier back and forth with great ease. As an engineer and management graduate, I found a new wisdom in subjects that I had earlier approached with great scepticism. The author's great gift was that he was able to talk of complex metaphysical ideas in simple terms that could be grasped by almost anyone with sufficient interest in the subject.

The author showed a great insight into the path of self-development traversed by mystics, saints and other people of high spiritual attainment. And he was enthusiastic about communicating this wisdom to his students. In the late eighties, the author developed a step-by-step correspondence course that very systematically takes the aspiring student through the various stages of spiritual development. The goal was to take people with deep interest in spirituality and intellectual ability, but with no qualification in philosophical or religious study, and establish them on the spiritual path. The course was practice based. It gave a deep insight into the various resistances that people face while attempting to change their mindset and animal nature. It has evolved in terms of increasing clarity over the last twenty years, and it forms much of the intellectual foundation of the present work.

In 1982, I left for the U.S. with the intention of pursuing higher studies. After many years I settled into a career in investment management in New York City. During that time, I also made it a point to seek out people who had an abiding interest in spiritual development. I also exchanged ideas with them. This group gradually expanded in size, and in the late nineties, I could invite the author to visit New York to conduct some spiritual awareness workshops. These workshops have taken a life of their own over the last fifteen years. They have improved in clarity of ideas and refinement. It was the prodding and encouragement of this group that made the author create this present work.

In my opinion, the present work is truly unique in that I am not aware of any other author who has written so directly on the subject of mysticism in this way. He has a signature style of conveying his message, which is striking, insightful and always to the point. The book is a wonderful piece of work – it is very well organized, the ideas come through with great clarity, and the message unfolds in a step-by-step manner. The whole work emphasizes practical application and does not digress into speculative scholarly discussions. The objective is to provide an insight into the practice, and to give aphorisms that crystallise the practice. These ideas are further expanded upon and clarified through insightful notes.

In explaining what mysticism is all about, the author elaborates on the idea of the human soul and its centrality to the process of transforming the human psychology. It does require a starting point, namely, a belief in the existence of a reality that is higher and greater than the human mind. Without this belief, or if there is entrenched scepticism about it, the aspirant will not be able to make the necessary spiritual connections that are necessary to have a breakthrough.

Going further, the author makes a distinction between the soul and the mind. The soul is a formation of consciousness that carries the seed of the universal spirit or God consciousness. Therefore it is said to be the source of our intuition, our conscience and our good intentions. From the spiritual point of view the mind is more like a tool or a servant that should be following our orders and working out the details. However, until this inner relationship is set, the mind marches to its own beat, dominating our psychology through ego, and drowning the feeble voice of the soul.

In this condition we are captivated and enslaved by the desires and cravings of our mind and body, and we ignore the call to follow higher ideals and live spiritually. Our personal agenda becomes all important and we fall into habits and patterns of thinking that keep us bound to our sensual or egoistic nature. Hence, we cannot perceive higher principles and the unity of consciousness that underlies all sentient beings.

The great contribution of this book is that it shows us how to bring the intangible reality called the soul forward in our life. It is by reversing our attention from the mind and body and turning it towards a spiritual reality. The aim is to become free from mental precepts and domination by ego.

© 2011-2018, Prashant S. Shah

The internal symbolism used in the book is easy to understand, but its proper implementation and application is challenging. Implementation forms the bulk of the subject matter of the book. It develops clarity in perception, gives us the criteria to choose from alternatives, and it shows us how to do all this without being compelled by the cravings and desires of our personal nature.

It is rare to find a work that is simultaneously insightful, inspiring and extremely practical. The author writes from a very keen understanding of his subject. He not only provides insights in the logical and stepwise fashion of a scientist, but he actually reveals the deeper mysteries of the inner life.

The author's style of writing is concise, intense and striking; so I advise the reader to pause frequently to reflect on the ideas while reading them.

The book can be read by anyone who wants a deeper understanding of human psychology and perception, but it would be most useful to the person who is actually travelling on the mystical path.

Madanda G. Machayya, Ph.D.
New York, January 2011

© 2011-2018, Prashant S. Shah

What is Mysticism?

1. Just as all the planets carry the light of the Sun in their own characteristic way, the individual human soul also carries the vibration of the Over-Soul or God.

Insightful Notes:

The Over Soul is the Lord or God. It is not an abstract concept, but a reality on the inner plane. Since the soul carries the God Presence, we can call it our 'God portion'. The God of the cosmos is wholly present in a seed form in the human soul.

Consciousness is the same in the cosmos and the individual. However, in the individual it is in an undeveloped condition or in the sleep state. The soul grows through our experiences on earth, and the qualities it develops are of a divine being.

2. The Over-Soul is also the Soul of humanity. It is intelligent, loving and caring. It guides us and inspires us, and nurtures our spiritual aspirations through our individual soul. However, the soul is not directly involved in our worldly affairs. It acts from

behind a veil. Hence, normally we are unaware of the presence of the soul.

Insightful Notes:

The world is an extension of God's being. You are an individualised expression of God under the conditions of time, space and matter. When consciousness is not associated with any form, it is God consciousness. But the consciousness in you is attached to your mind and body (which are your instruments for functioning on earth). Hence, in the present condition you are unaware of God and the soul (your God portion).

When consciousness is attached to your mind and body, you feel that you are just a mind with a body, and not a greater being like a soul. Then your power of consciousness is contracted, and you think and act as an individual whose interests' conflict with the interest of others. As a result you do not experience your unity in consciousness.

3. Mysticism is the art of becoming aware of the God Presence in our soul and bringing it forward in our life. We do it by learning to live for the sake of the soul and not merely for the sake of our mind and body.

© 2011-2018, Prashant S. Shah

Insightful Notes:

When you are unaware of the soul, you identify with the mind and body. It causes you to assume the identity of a 'mental-self' – the false self, which is the basis of the ego. Further, you live to uphold this mental-self. Hence, it conditions all your perceptions. It gives rise to your personal focus, and to a world that is coloured by your fears, desires and personal ambitions. Just as your skin separates your body from everything else, the mental-self separates you from the Universal Consciousness or God.

According to mysticism, this separation has given rise to 'a fall' or the lowering in the state of your consciousness. Hence, to 'rise' or lift the state of your consciousness, you have to come out of your false identification with the mental-self. You do not have to overcome all the imperfections of your individual nature; you have to only come out of the confines of the mental-self.

Thus, the main task in mysticism is to bring the soul or the God element forward in your life. Then you can live for the sake of the soul and not merely for the desires and tendencies in the mind and body.

© 2011-2018, Prashant S. Shah

4.   The practice of mysticism begins with merely a belief in the existence of a reality that is higher and greater than the human mind. We install it as a Deity in our mind. Then we begin to relate with it. We dwell upon its image, call its presence and arouse our feelings for it.

Gradually the image becomes alive, and begins to respond to us and guide us. Ultimately the Deity becomes a divine presence that we can attune with at will. In this way the Deity serves as a seed for our spiritual practice.

Insightful Notes:
First, you plant a seed of the God-idea in your mind. Next, you nurture this seed with your love and devotion. Then, the 'soul element' begins to sprout in your mind. It opens a window in the mind, and through this window you can begin to see and experience realities that are somewhat beyond the scope of your mental horizon.

5.   The idea of the Deity in mysticism should not be confused with the concept of God that is advocated by organised religion.

It is not the idol that is worshipped in the temples, churches or places of worship. It is more like a divine presence that resides within our soul and shows us the ways of the higher consciousness.

Insightful Notes:

In mysticism, you do not learn a set of customs, rituals and invocations. Instead, you learn how to connect up with the God Presence that resides in your soul, and how to be lead by it. Thus, there is no need for a priest or rituals. The need, if any, is for a personal guide. Hence, we say: *"The saints derive their wisdom directly from God, but the scholars learn it from each other. Thus, the scholars replace the wisdom of God with the opinion of the people."*

When you learn from a preacher (particularly in the modern times), it is like one blind man leading another. The role of a spiritual guide is different. His (or her) task is to help you in making your own personal connection with the God Consciousness. Here 'learnt up' or scholarly knowledge is not sufficient. The guide must have some attainment. He must be able to perceive the truth in matters of life directly, without having to infer them with the mind. Otherwise he cannot have the ability to deal with the numerous deceptions and pitfalls that arise on the spiritual path.

People are unable to differentiate between the term Gods that you make offerings to for deriving worldly benefits as in pooja, and the term Deity as used in spiritual practice sadhana. Just as there are souls and an Over-Soul, there are Gods and God in the cosmos. The term 'GODS' is normally used to refer to universal beings or personalities with individuality. They preside over particular functions in the cosmos. They also carry the divine element, but unlike God their powers are limited to the function they have to perform.

Human beings are not Gods. However, a human being can attain to the plane of Gods. This is because the human soul has the God Presence. The soul grows on its own plane through the experiences of our life on earth, and ultimately becomes a self-conscious being with a body of light. This luminous being has the same status as other Gods, Angels or Devas in the cosmos.

Just as there are Gods or Devas in manifestation, there are also Demons or Asuras and Rakshasas.

These are nature's products. They have been put out in the cosmos to serve certain purposes or functions. In the spiritual context their main purpose is to test human beings and provide the conditions of resistance that is necessary for certain kinds of developments.

THE PRACTICE

There are four stages to the practice.

1.   First, you INSTALL a Deity in the mind: You choose a divine image. You concentrate on it, and feed it with your love and devotion. Then you begin to relate with it.

Insightful Notes:

Academic philosophy teaches you concepts of life, whereas mysticism teaches you the art of nurturing the soul. Thus, mysticism is a practical philosophy. It is more like a practice with a philosophy. It shows you what you need to do and why you should do it.

You begin by choosing a divine image — an image of a Deity with a human form that you find inspiring. It may be a picture of a traditional Godhead, an angel, a master, or even a person through whom you had experienced selfless love.

Then you set the image in your mind. You gaze at a picture of it for a few minutes every day and try to visualise it – you try to see something of it with your closed eyes. If you find that difficult to do, just imagine that your Deity is present in front of you.

Then mentally relate with your Deity just as you would relate with a dear friend.

2. Second, you begin to ATTUNE your mind with the Deity and try to perceive the ways of the Over-Soul. You listen to the silent promptings and the indications that arise as you hold on to the divine presence.

Insightful Notes:

Once you can visualise the Deity's image, you have to practice it often and make it reality in your life. Then you can call God's presence in your mind and use it to clarify your thoughts, emotions and motives. In this way you align the forces in your mind with the ways of a higher consciousness. Gradually your mind will become receptive, and you will begin to see the different way in which the higher consciousness works.

God's ways and our ego's ways are usually different. Hence, when you put a matter before the Deity, newer options and alternatives arise in your mind. Earlier your predispositions decided for you, but now you can see different possibilities. Hence, you have a choice. And what you choose always makes a difference in your life.

3. Third, you try to FOLLOW the guidance or message that you have received. As you do this your motives get purified, your understanding becomes clear, and you develop a subtle insight into life.

Insightful Notes:

This is always the hardest part. Understanding concepts is easy, but changing your habits and ways of doing things is always difficult.

Difficulties arise because your tendencies are largely rooted in the subconscious portion of the mind. You can see the forces in your conscious mind, and so you can deal with the forces there. But you cannot clearly observe the forces in the subconscious portion of the mind. Hence, you find it difficult to handle these forces.

However, first you handle the forces in your conscious mind. Then you find that they have some roots in the subconscious. You try to carefully find the roots and try to uproot them.

If you succeed in overcoming even a small tendency, it is a big success. Your tendency will get weaker and your will power will get stronger. The force held by the tendency gets transferred onto your will. Then it becomes easier for you to overcome other tendencies. However, the reverse is also true. If you fail, you break your will power. Then it becomes easier to fail again. So you have to be very careful. Start by winning and continue to win. The small victories will add up.

You have to just trust the higher consciousness and allow it to show you what you need to do and how you should do it. Gradually you can overcome many of the rebellious tendencies in your nature and develop self-control. Then you can go further and try to have a breakthrough.

4. Fourth, you begin to GIVE YOURSELF to the Deity. You allow the Deity to dominate your awareness, to remake your nature, and to use it for a greater purpose.

Insightful Notes:

Many people fear the Deity thinking that it is like another person who can exploit them. However, the Deity is only a spiritual entity that takes shape within your awareness. It is your connection with the God Presence that dwells in your soul. Hence, the process of giving yourself is merely taking away the power from your ego and giving it to the higher consciousness.

You make your mind follow the ways of the higher consciousness, and it will totally change the way in which you think, feel and do things. Ultimately you have to make God the **doer** in your life. The saying is: *"Be God's alone; for if you are God's then God will be yours."*

THE BASIC TASK

1.   The basic task in mysticism is to ESTABLISH your connection with the Deity. To do that you focus on the divine image and try to feel the divine presence.

This ability greatly improves with practice. Once you can experience the divine presence, you can begin to put your decisions and difficulties before the Deity and allow it to guide you.

Insightful Notes:

The people who have a materialistic attitude to life continue to debate whether a person has a soul or not. However, the soul is something that cannot be proved objectively. You prove it to yourself subjectively by making the Divine Presence the doer in your life. Then God will bring the soul forward in your life.

Thus, the inner being, the soul, has to be unveiled. It is an inner experience, which by itself is a great achievement. And this achievement is not something you can get by merely asking for it. You have to discover this by yourself; and no one can do it for you.

The soul has an identity that is different from the identity of your mind and body. And the proof of its awakening is in the radical change in your outlook, insight and state of your being.

What is the practice? First you select a Deity. You select two things: A God Idea' and a 'God Form'.

The God idea is the Mystic's method of making the higher states of consciousness intelligible to your limited mental consciousness. It creates an opening in your mind — through which you can receive the love and guidance from above.

The saying is: *"First make God a reality in your life; then your self-made God will lead you to the higher states of consciousness."* Thus, the God idea is used to make an opening in the mind through which you can receive spiritual influence.

When you want to make God a reality in your life, God cannot be allowed to remain an abstract principle. It has to be something concrete that you can feel for and relate with. For this purpose you have to select a God form. It gives you the practical means by which you can hold the spiritual presence in your mind. You use it in the same way as you use a spoon to drink your soup. Further, it is easier to relate with a human image. Hence, the mystics want you to select a God form with a human face.

Whereas a God idea is used to lift the motives and the quality of your life, the God form is used to provide you with the practical means for doing your concentration and contemplation practice. You can consider the form as a vessel into which you can receive the higher truths and power.

For all practical purposes the Deity is your personal God with a God idea and a God form. Thus, God in the form of a Deity will serve you as a 'complete channel' for doing your spiritual practice. In mysticism you use it to actualise the divine presence in your mind. It will establish your direct and personal relationship with the God.

2. You can call the Deity daily in your meditation and clarify your mind in its presence. You can call its presence as you attend to the situations that arise in your everyday life. And you can seek its approval before confirming your decisions.

© 2011-2018, Prashant S. Shah

In this way you make the Deity your INNER COMPANION and become fond of it. It will love you, guide you, and help you in managing your affairs.

Insightful Notes:

You dwell on the Deity to open your mind to a higher influence. A simple practice is to put all your decisions before the Deity and ask for approval.

First you ask; then you wait for the indications to arise. You know it is an indication when you recognise it as 'something different' that has arisen in your mind. When the indication is true, you feel enthusiastic about following it.

Often you don't get any indication. It could be that the conditions are not agreeable; some things have to happen first; perhaps there are contradictory forces at play; or maybe you are just not open to the real options. Whatever the reason, if you look for it sincerely you will find it. You have to correct the mistake and then ask again.

As you use this method you not only get directions in matters of life, but it will build your personal relationship with the Deity. Hence, you must use it often.

3. The Deity is SYMBOLIC of a cosmic principle that is powerful, great and all-abiding. And yet it is something that is connected with you, loves you and cares for you.

The Deity knows your situation, your capacity, your nature, your circumstances, and what is best for you. Hence, your spiritual task is to simply keep up your inner companionship with the Deity and to sincerely try and follow the silent promptings or indications that arise.

Insightful Notes:

The practice of frequently dwelling on the Deity, your personal God, with the object of attuning your mind with it is called 'contemplation'. Here, the concentration practice is not intense or for long durations. You concentrate on the Deity for short durations, but you do it more often.

A typical practice is to simply remember the Deity before you start any activity. Just feel its presence and start. As you advance in this practice a portion of your awareness will remain attuned with the Deity and the other portion will carry out the work. Then the Deity will oversee the task as you carry it out. Then the right things begin to happen through you.

4. On this path DIFFICULTIES will arise. They happen due to your egoistic considerations. You may overreact to the circumstances, to the events, to the people around you, and to the conditions under which you have to live.

Insightful Notes:

Most people ask God to grant their wishes or to support them even when they continue to act with egoistic considerations. However, in mysticism you contemplate on God to impose the higher way in your mind.

What happens when you do the opposite? That is when you try to impose your mental processes or desires on the higher consciousness? Then you get disconnected. The Deity simply withdraws and the ego comes in to deceive you. Then the message you receive will more often be an echo of your wishes or secret desires. Hence, you have to be careful.

5.   Your task in mysticism is not to try and sort out the difficulties by yourself through mental effort, but to INVOLVE the Deity in sorting them out. Whenever a difficulty arises, simply put it before the Deity. Then wait for the indications and try to follow them.

Insightful Notes:

When you involve the Deity in your affairs, you don't pull the higher consciousness down to your level. Instead, you use the higher consciousness to lift yourself (your nature) up. You have to use the opportunities you get in life to impose the higher way in your mind.

In addition, when you do things in this way, you generate 'higher level solutions'. The solutions will be more inclusive, more harmonious, and hence also more effective.

6.   You have to keep the TRUST that the guidance that you receive, despite the

appearances and your doubts, is the right thing to do or the way out of your difficulty.

Insightful Notes:

The Deity consciousness never orders, dictates or interferes. It never insists. It only quietly points out, shows or indicates. For this reason, the Deity is called *'the silent master'*. It mirrors your thoughts and actions and shows them up for what they really are; it shows you their significance.

You have to trust in the indications that arise. The Deity shows the truth or the way, but what you do with it depends on you, on what you decide to do. So, when you follow the indications don't interpret them with wishful or egoistic thinking. You have to be careful not to deceive yourself.

THE INNER WORK

1. Once your connection with the Deity is established, you can take up the task of CLEANSING and reorganising your life. The defects in your nature will get reflected in the situations of your life.

Your task is to use the Deity to see your mistakes, to know the correct way, and to follow the truth at every point of choice.

Insightful Notes:
What exactly is the work of purification or inner cleaning? It is mainly the work of adjusting your beliefs and attitudes according to the higher consciousness. You have to look into your mindset, find the faults in it, and correct them. It will release you from compulsive habits and tendencies that bind your awareness to the lower levels of consciousness.

In mysticism you do this inner work by involving the Deity in your life.

2.   Usually the indications you receive are simple, but they may not be easy to follow. Difficulties arise due to resistance from within you. There are many things inside your nature that do not want to change. Your mindset, your vital nature, and your personal habits will RESIST changing. Hence, for some time you may struggle.

Insightful Notes:

Adjusting the mindset and breaking habits is neither easy nor appealing. And this task becomes more difficult when you consider this task as unnecessary — that is when you refuse to consider the habits as a fault!

Your mindset and habits have been formed out of your past experiences. These experiences were interpreted by your mental-self or ego. In spiritual life you have to reset them according to the ways of the higher consciousness.

3.   However, you can have spiritual attainment in some degree of fullness only AFTER you overcome the inner opponents. You cannot avoid them, and nobody else can accomplish this task for you.

Insightful Notes:

The basic nature of the mental-self (which is the root of our egoistic tendencies) is to push you downwards by justifying your animal inclinations. And the basic nature of the soul is to lift you upwards by awakening your virtues. Both these natures are within you.

People can gift you with information and material things, but the inner work of understanding and organising your forces around the soul is something that you have to do by yourself! You cannot bypass this task and no other person can do it for you.

4. The spiritual practice at this stage will really test you. You have to unlearn the wrong ways; reject what is false; and correct your assumptions. In mysticism all this begins to happen naturally as you try to IMPOSE the way of the Deity in your mind.

Insightful Notes:

In Raja Yoga the spiritual practice requires you to do extensive introspection with a disinterested mind. It makes you aware of the faults in your mindset and the impurities in your nature. Then you track them down the roots. You have to carefully break all the connections that maintain these impurities in your nature. You have to reject everything that resists the change you want to bring about. This is a tough task; it requires a lot of doing; and it is filled with many dangers and deceptions.

However, the practice in mysticism is much simpler. Here you remember the Deity and focus on its presence, and it will automatically show up the wrong movements. Then you ask the Deity and it will show you what is proper, appropriate or necessary in the situation. Then your only task is to impose the higher way in your mind.

Once the higher consciousness is involved in your life, you have to simply keep your mind open to it and allow it to guide your actions. Then your actions will autocorrect and you can also find the right movements in society.

5. As you progress, your values and motives change. Your actions become more harmonious, and the conditions of your life also improve.

Gradually the FOCUS of your life begins to change. Instead of being a charmer of the mind and body, now you become a server of

the universal consciousness that underlies them.

Insightful Notes:

In the early stages of spiritual practice you need personal incentives to do things or to seek things. But as you mature, you are happy to just stay with God and do things for their own sake.

When you can mirror a higher consciousness, it will be easier to find the right things to do and to get cooperation from others. Normally 'cooperation' is something the ego does not go in for unless there is a secondary agenda. The higher consciousness, however, is inclusive — it always includes the concerns of other people. Hence, the solutions that arise by involving the higher influence get easily accepted by others.

Once you make your mind a server of the higher consciousness, you get released from the prison of your personal thoughts and emotions. You can rest in the calm, wide, and loving consciousness of the soul, and simply take your joy from doing what needs to be done.

6. Once the soul has come forward in your life, you can reflect the ways of the Over Soul. Then you experience kindness, insight and understanding.

Insightful Notes:

Your soul carries the seed of the Over Soul. So when the seed sprouts, spiritual qualities arise in you naturally. The qualities like kindness, unity, and fair play begin to arise in you naturally.

Gradually you begin to see a higher purpose to your life. You develop a spiritual attitude, which is a particular mental and emotional attitude towards higher ideals and God.

7. Your mind will not be restless. It will be calm and alert, and your intuition will become RELIABLE. You begin to see things clearly, without projecting your wishes, fears or tendencies on them.

Insightful Notes:

With the mental consciousness you can only know things indirectly; by inferring, interpreting and decoding them. However, life matters are complex. There is no single cause or effect relationship. There are many levels of causes and effects, and they interact. Hence, logic is useless.

So, when you function exclusively with the mind, you cannot recognise what is true – you only know what could be or may be or should be true. Thus, when you perceive exclusively with the mind you can easily get confused, deceived and deluded.

In contrast the Higher Consciousness is an intelligent principle. It has many sided awareness and the power to discriminate in matters of life. Hence, when you see with the higher consciousness, you don't need language, the aid of sense impressions, or inferences to know. You get a 'truth sense' that directly shows what is true and also tells how true it really is. Hence, your perceptions will not be limited to inferences.

8.   Gradually the desires and the tendencies of the mind begin to LOSE THEIR HOLD over you. Then you can accept the situations of life as they arrive. You consider them as outcomes or value-neutral events. Hence, you can deal with them appropriately, without having to react.

© 2011-2018, Prashant S. Shah

Insightful Notes:

It is the mental-self or the ego that experiences hurt, insult, hatred, jealousy, etc. It craves for esteem and has insatiable greed. So, when this fellow becomes objective in your mind, you are released from its reactions (emotions). Then you can go along with the flow of life and accept what life offers.

What happens when the ego dominates? You feel valued for only what you can do or give; there is an absence of love; and little things do not cheer you.

Then you can get some temporary happiness, but the inner conditions that sustain happiness do not exist. So, sooner or later your mind will gravitate towards restlessness and dissatisfaction.

The Practical Side of Purification

a) Purifying the mind from thoughts

Your mind is an open territory for thoughts. Thoughts can dip into your mind and cast their image. If you give attention to the image, you feed it. Then it visits your mind more frequently to feed on your attention. However, if you don't give it your attention, it has to leave. When the mind is in a passive condition, a continuous stream of chatter goes on in the mind.

However, when you practice concentration, you get the power to WITHHOLD your attention from thoughts. Then a thought can still dip into your mind, but it cannot stay there unless you allow it to stay.

If you can keep your mind in a withheld condition, you can simply observe the flow of thoughts – thoughts coming in and going out. You can see what attracts them to visit, and the message they have for you. If you don't attend to the thought, it has to pass by without causing any disturbance in your mind.

The thoughts that visit you frequently are connected with your desires or what you are trying to do. Others are a clutter of useless personal thoughts, like mental replays. You can get rid of these personal thoughts by simply looking away from them. You can also do it by displacing them. It will be enough to remember your mantra or focus on your Deity.

When your attention is not dragged by thoughts a quiet enjoyment arises. The mind becomes calm and alert.

b) Purifying the mind from emotions

Emotions dip into your mind to feed on your vital energy. If you give them your attention they get their feed (like birds) and come back again and again.

These emotions are like 'cunning animals with a primitive intelligence'. They just want to survive, and to do that they need food. They can easily draw on your vital energy when you are disturbed. The disturbed energy is compatible with their vibration and so it is excellent food for them.

The emotions that you entertain keep a vital hold over you. They control your behaviour. And when you are under their influence you don't want your misery to end. Something inside you enjoys this sadness! And if other people join with you, you can also make them miserable.

However, when you stand back from an emotion, you objectify it. Then you can look upon it as a parasite that wants to feed on your vitality.

The next step is to develop an aversion in your mind for this emotion. If you do it properly, you can reject the emotion in the same way as you rejected thoughts. The only difference in dealing with emotions is that they stir up a lot of agitation in the mind.

The emotions are your self-created demons that you have been feeding for years. They are not going to leave you without putting up a fight. They can make you feel that a life without them will be unexciting and not worth living. And if you sympathise with them they will break your resolution and make you give in.

© 2011-2018, Prashant S. Shah

So, before you take up the battle with an emotion, you must create an aversion for having it. If you consider it is nice to have the emotion, you cannot overcome it. Then further, you should remember your Deity and seek its help in overcoming the emotion.

There will be a bitter battle in your mind. However, the emotion is never something you cannot overcome. There is a lot of difference between: "you can't do it" and "you won't do it". The truth is that you can always do it, but more often you won't do it. However, when you succeed here, you will be really worth something spiritually.

c) Purification in the body

The emotional energies in your mind have an access to the endocrinal glands in the body. Hence, the cleansing process is accompanied by some hormonal disturbance in the body. Further, if an emotion has been around from a long time, some disturbances have settled in the body. Then there will also be some toxins that have to be expelled.

So cleansing the emotions is often accompanied by functional disturbances such as the irritable bowel syndrome, and respiratory and skin allergies. However, these disorders do not need medical treatment. When you are sufficiently cleansed the symptoms will go away.

When certain deep rooted 'vasanas' (tendencies inherited from the past) are being thrown out you can expect some serious mood changes. Hostile thoughts, unnatural sexual urges, continuous anger without cause, or a deep depression can arise. Again, you don't need therapeutic treatment. As the tendencies leave the mind, the symptoms leave the body, and you come out much cleaner.

d) On correcting your mistakes

Everyone makes mistakes. But when you perceive the mistake egoistically, you become defensive. Then you cannot admit it *as your mistake*. You think that by admitting it your self-image will get tainted. Then further, if your self-worth is already low, admitting the mistake can lower it further. And so the experience can be very painful.

So you desperately try to cover up the mistake or refuse to consider the mistake as the result of your faulty response. In either case, the cause of the mistake remains. So the mistake repeats, and you continue to suffer the consequences.

However, if you admit the mistake, you can find the fault in your mindset that is causing it. Then instead of defending or justifying your mistake you can find the ways to correct it. You have to correct the tendency in your mindset that is actually causing the mistake in your life. When you do that your nature gets transformed and you also don't make the mistake.

Transformation

1. Once the higher consciousness has become your guiding light, your spiritual quest begins to take a big turn. It no longer remains your personal endeavour for your personal profit. You begin to give up the expectation that your image or ego should be the main beneficiary from what you do.

Insightful Notes:

In the beginning of your spiritual pursuit your attitude will be egocentric. You live mainly to satisfy the desires in the mind and body. Hence, you consider your spiritual practice to be your personal endeavour, for your personal profit. You expect that your mental-self, formed out of your personal thoughts, preferences, desires and impulses, should gain in strength and get recognition. Without this initial expectation you may lack the necessary motivation to undertake the spiritual journey.

2. You painfully realise that instead of reinforcing your personality, the spiritual practice is going to SUBORDINATE IT to a

higher principle that is being awakened inside you. Something that is truly great is beginning to find its expression through your personality.

Insightful Notes:

As you progress, you are increasingly led by the promptings of the Deity, and you rely less on your personal ability and worldly contacts. You have to be quick to understand that the Deity will sustain all your personal needs, *but not your egoistic or vital demands.* There are some things you are not going to get — they are simply not for you. You have to just outgrow the desire for having them. If you continue to crave for such things, you generate serious contradictions in your mind. It will upset your spiritual pursuit.

Why is this experience very painful? The biggest emotional entity in your mind is the mental-self. It is sentimental and gets deep vital satisfaction (like the sexual satisfaction) by feeding on your disturbed energy. It upholds the vital habits of self-pity and it can even cause you to make a virtue out of your suffering! However, it will shirk when you begin to give up taking vital delight by living spiritually.

On the other hand, if you give the mental self a 'free play' it will enslave you. Then your spiritual pursuit is as good as discarded. It takes some maturing to see these emotional entities for what they really are. Only after you do that you can generate the will power that is necessary to overcome them.

3. At this stage of practice you are able to attune with the Deity by merely dwelling upon its image. You are happy to be with the Deity; to serve it; and to experience its love.

Insightful Notes:

In the beginning the mental-self interprets your experiences. It generates a continuous mental talk, telling you what is good for you or bad for you. Or it can project its wishes or fears upon the events of life. However if you indulge in such personal interpretations, they will maintain divisions within your consciousness and create inner conflicts.

When you practice living for God this activity of the mental-self gets replaced by the quiet and disinterested action prompted by the soul. You prefer to keep your mind in a withheld state instead of indulging in useless thinking or becoming occupied with unnecessary wants and have-to-do's.

© 2011-2018, Prashant S. Shah

It is often asked: *What is the difference between human love and God's Love?*

Getting married, having a family, becoming a member of a community, keeping a pet, etc. are ways of experiencing love in society. Your partner, family, relatives, friends, enemies, etc. are all given to you for playing your roles in the drama of life on earth. So, you have to play your part and try to enjoy the love you can get.

However, human love is egoistic, conditional and temporary. The ego keeps expectations and calculates the 'give and take' in relationships. So the love you get from human beings will be selfish, fragile and conditional.

On the other hand the love you get from God is unconditional and lasting; it is like nectar. In the presence of this love the 'ego sense' evaporates, and the mind enlarges. Then you feel the world is your family and you have a duty towards this larger family.

4.   Your actions are no longer driven by egoistic considerations, and you are able to impose the higher way in your mind.

Gradually a divine presence begins to SETTLE inside you.

Insightful Notes:

To stay aware of God, you have to focus your attention more on being and less on doing things. When you keep your focus on serving God, the contents of your mind, the thoughts, emotions and memories, take on an objective existence. It removes restlessness and discontent from your life. You don't feel you have 'to do something' to be peaceful or happy!

When you keep your hold on the Deity, the higher consciousness begins to take over your mind. Then your thoughts and feelings will serve the soul and not the ego.

So, first you create the conditions that allow you to remain connected with the Deity. Then you abandon the mental-self and let the Deity work in you *as it wants to*. You particularly look away from your personal thoughts and selfish considerations.

Then you experience the Deity consciousness. It is a joyful STATE and not just a feeling. It is only when you get disconnected from this state that you crave for happiness through sensations and interaction with other people.

5a. Many times during this practice your awareness flows into the divine presence that is behind the mind.

Insightful Notes:

As you progress, your will gets transferred onto the divine image (presence) that you dwell on. It gives rise to a spiritual being within your consciousness. Something separates from you and joins the Deity. Then you can experience the Deity objectively as a living spiritual image within your awareness.

In mysticism God is not a separate person. There is no Mr. or Ms. God. The God image that you visualise is a divine image of a Deity that was perhaps used by some saint. Now it is a spiritual entity on the higher plane and it is connected with you; it has a presence within your consciousness.

5b. It gives you the feeling that there is just one being, which is watching itself through the eyes of different observers.

Insightful Notes:

Your soul carries the seed of God consciousness. And the God consciousness is in the soul of all beings. Hence, the experience of this consciousness also gives you the experience of the unity. In particular, you feel that all human beings are related; they are like the children of the same father; that things on earth are for everyone and not just for you and your family. You know that other people on earth are your fellows, and that each person is going to return to the same destination. Hence, you feel love for them.

When the soul comes forward an overseeing consciousness arises, which is totally detached from worldliness. It sees the tossing in the mind, but it is and not affected by any happening in the world.

5c.   You can see the potential in every person, and know what drives them to act. You feel that everyone is doing the best they can from their level, and hence you can be patient and sympathetic with them.

Insightful Notes:

When you see everything with the soul consciousness, your concern enlarges to include others. Then you can inwardly connect with them and experience their thoughts, feelings, motives and situations as if they are your own.

However, you do not compel others with your vision. They have to come to understand and accept things on their own.

6. Once you experience the soul you know it is not of this world. Your personality, which is like a shadow, is here; and earlier you had mistaken the shadow for the reality.

Insightful Notes:

There is someone who looks after you from behind a curtain. It is your true person. Your personality is a formation that you use to carry out your actions on earth. But intrinsically, it is like a shadow. As long as your attention is exclusively turned outward, towards the world, you mistake the shadow for the reality. However, once you know what is true, you cannot be the same as before.

7. Now you can see the falsehoods of the mental processes and the ignorance of being led by the mind. Even the moral sense is

transcended, and you see both the right and wrong as ignorant mental inferences.

Insightful Notes:

The eye of the soul sees everything in the context of a much greater picture. Hence, once the soul has awakened in your life you do not easily misunderstand things. You do not push to make things happen; but you are willing to wait for the necessary conditions or the inner situation to arise. You do not get lost in 'role playing' or in chasing mind-made images. You consider them to be merely the projections of fears and desires of the mental-self. You don't feel driven to do anything.

8a. Once the inner being is awake, the events in the outer world lose their seriousness for you. Your life on earth becomes like a play wherein the outcomes do not really matter.

Insightful Notes:

Once you have discovered your identity as a soul, the charm of pursuing mental attainments, sensual desires or personal glory is lost. You can only pursue these things when you disconnect from the soul. Hence, you do not crave to become an important person like a Napoleon, an Alexander, a billionaire, a beauty queen, or the President of USA!

Ignorant people keep on increasing their worldly and religious activities. They do it because they fear poverty, uncertainty, or their opponents. However, the mystic will say: *"Devote yourself entirely to God and then see the marvels. God is the greatest power. Hence, when you belong to God, the entire cosmos with all its contents belongs to you!"*

When you understand this saying, you will not remain preoccupied with worldly activities. Instead, you will spend more time with God. The mystics say: *"Let other people have their affairs, but let your affair be with God."* The needs of ordinary people are fulfilled by giving attention to their material needs, whereas the needs of spiritual aspirers are fulfilled by contemplating on God. Remember the assurances God has given through his saints:

"Remember Me and I will remember you."

"I am always near to those who call upon Me."

"If you look to Me, I will certainly look to you."

"If you take two steps towards Me, I will take four steps towards you."

8b.   Now you can carry on the work of transforming your nature, of helping others, of world repair, etc. or you can withdraw into the wider and peaceful consciousness that is beyond the mind.

Insightful Notes:

Is there a difference between changing your attitude and transforming it? In spiritual life transformation is much more than changing the attitude. It is not merely making some adjustments in your mindset. Your whole nature has to be re-casted in the mould of your realisation.

You have to persistently remove everything in your nature that contradicts or protests against the higher consciousness. When you do it sufficiently, transformation happens. And when that happens, you are not the same as before. Something within you disappears and something new arises in its place, which is totally different from what you had known.

How does the goal of helping others or doing 'world repair' fit in? The experience of the soul tells you that there is a greater power, an over-soul or the Lord. It is the Self of all. When you experience its influence, you really want to serve this Great One. You want to become a channel for bringing the highest influence into the world.

However, first you have to anchor the God consciousness in yourself. Thereafter you can become a 'spiritual worker' and serve to anchor the higher consciousness in the world. And to do that you have to simply serve the truth and allow the necessary work to be done through you.

THE MESSAGE

You can practice meditation and begin to experience some stillness in the mind; you can practice devotion and begin to enjoy ecstasy of the emotional experience; you can practice breathing techniques and experience vitality in the body; but if the soul has not come forward in your life, truly nothing lasting has been attained!

Insightful Notes:

In mysticism you pursue God. But God has a presence in the soul. Hence, by contemplating on God you bring the soul forward in your life.

The soul is a luminous being that lives on the spiritual plane. It supports your personality here on earth. The personality, on the other hand, is a formation of nature. It functions and grows under the conditions of dependency and struggle.

The soul continues its long association with the personality, forming it afresh with each existence, but maintains its continuity with its past. The aim of this soul's long association with our nature is to develop a 'spiritual body' — something in nature that is totally responsive to the soul. Then soul can use this formation to have a higher existence in the inner worlds.

At a certain stage in your pursuit your attention gets internalised. Then you, as nature (prakruti), become aware of the soul. This ancient one is a luminous being that has always been there. It was watching over you from behind a veil; but now that you have reversed your gaze from the outer world you have found it. The soul will thrill you with its love and beauty; and give you the experience of deep love that cannot be got from people or things of the world.

The soul is the purpose of your life on earth. So, when it awakens everything in your life begins to find its proper place: You know what you have come to do; you get the opportunities that you really need; and other things do not matter very much.

When the soul comes forward in your life newer faculties arise within you. Then you are not limited to the intellectual process of inferring and figuring things out in matters of life. You can directly receive a subtle radiation from the soul. It will inform you, caution you, guide you, and also grant your wishes.

APHORISMS

For Awakening the Soul

Here are some aphorisms that will guide you through the difficulties on the path of mysticism. The word 'God' is used instead of 'the Deity' so that these Aphorisms can be used by anyone.

Insightful Notes:

In spiritual practice there is a lot of repetition. We do the same things over and over again until they are completely done. Often we succeed in working out something and think that our task is complete. However, our tendencies have many links in the subconscious. So the same tendencies re-present themselves in different forms. Then we have to work on them all over again.

The tendencies of our nature are have deep roots. Hence, they can be very obstinate. We cannot make some adjustments in a general way and expect to have lasting results. We have to work out everything in detail, from many sides, and at many levels. During this long period time we can use the aphorisms given below to keep your attention on the spiritual path. The results become permanent only after there is some transformation.

1. Call the presence of God

Sit in a quiet place with eyes closed and begin to think of God: Feel that someone is sustaining your breath; that someone is sitting beside you and watching you; that someone loves you and is seeking to guide you to find what you really want.

Do this practice daily until you have made space for God in your life. Then try to experience God's Presence. Allow the experience to lift you above your present circumstances and conditions, and create an atmosphere of peace and joy around you.

Insightful Notes:
This is the foundation exercise. All further practices are built around it. You have to put aside some time each day for God. If you miss this time, consider disciplining yourself by missing your next meal!

When you take up the practice of mysticism, you have to believe that the God consciousness is always there around you. The time and effort that you devote to your spiritual practice is for making your direct, one-on-one connection with God.

Just keep the God-thought in your mind and be patient. The seed will sprout. Then divine qualities will begin to arise in your nature.

2. Extend the spiritual feeling into your everyday life

Think that God is everywhere, behind all things, and is quietly guiding your actions. Hence, all you have to do is to become receptive to God's presence.

Wear something to remind you of God. Then, during the idle moments of the day, and at several other times also, dwell on that something and recall the feeling of peace and inner support.

Try to hold on to this experience as you proceed to carry out your tasks and duties in everyday life. It will add a spiritual quality to your work.

Insightful Notes:
When you do this exercise sincerely, your practice becomes dynamic — it becomes many sided. Then your progress will be rapid.

When you focus on the divine presence at many times during the day, your anxiety gets reduced (then thinking about the future does not project anxiety); and the mental replays (memories of past events) will not pester you. Then it will be easier for you to keep your mind open and receive intuition.

When you make this practice a habit, a spiritual presence will linger in the background of your mind and give you spiritual support.

3. Involve God in your life

Try to perceive the hand of God behind the intelligence, thoughts and actions of others. The more you keep up your inner companionship with God, the more clearly you notice the 'hand of God' behind all things.

Remember, God's grace for you will depend on how strongly you hold on to God.

Insightful Notes:

Whenever you come across a difficulty, do not try to figure it out through a mental exercise. Instead, refer it to God; and try to respond to the situation with God's help.

How can you do that? Simply ask God. Then keep your mind open and receptive to God's response. At some time during the day, or sometimes later on, you will suddenly become aware of what needs to be done.

Then don't run away with the little hint you have got. Continue to seek God's help in doing the task. From time to time look to God and ask God to guide your actions.

© 2011-2018, Prashant S. Shah

When this practice becomes a habit, you can work better, and the outcomes will not create tension or upset in your mind.

To establish the divine presence in your mind you have to increase your trust in God. To do this, you have to remain connected with God and depend on God. Then God will look after you.

However, if there is a lack of spiritual longing, God's response will also be hesitant.

4. Follow God

Trust God, communicate with God, and follow the silent promptings you receive from God.

When you perform the duties of your roles, do them without becoming greedy, jealous or fearful. Don't protest your situation, bear a grudge, or become disappointed.

When you keep up this practice something of your old nature will die every day, and something new from God will replace it. You have to only persist with this practice for a few years and your nature will be transformed beyond recognition.

Insightful Notes:

When you live for God's sake, you do not act for ego satisfaction. You become like the flower that does not see its own beauty and willingly gives its fragrance to others.

Hence, don't crave for appreciation from others. If others show their appreciation, don't let that make you proud.

When you are useful to others, consider that God is providing them help through you. Just focus on serving God and you will never lose your way on the mystic path.

You progress on this path by clearing the source of conflicts in your mind. These conflicts arise due to the tendencies you have inherited from your past. However, you don't use will power to straighten them out. Instead, you do it by involving God in your life. Just do your work and perform your duties while remembering God. That's all.

In doing this task you have to be very persistent. But people are fickle. They try one method and then try something else, and go on in this way. They are like people who try to find water by digging a little here and there. To find water you have to dig at one point and dig deep. In the same way, to find God you have to follow just one path and go far on it.

5. The attitude with which you do your work always matters

To God, your position and the nature of your work are unimportant. To God, the peace in your mind, the love in your heart and the spirit with which you do your work are important. What really matters is the attitude and motives with which you act.

Hence, always work through a mind that is kind, understanding and caring. Remember, it is better to do no work than to work through an agitated mind!

Insightful Notes:

From the spiritual point of view, your inner state decides how you act. Hence, how you act becomes more important than what you do.

The thoughts and feelings that you bring into the world through your actions are most important. Your spiritual task is to simply stay connected with the God and allow the higher intelligence to act through you.

Joy does not arise from what work you do; it arises from the inner state that you tap into while you are doing that work. Hence, it is not the specific action that gives you joy. It is the sense of aliveness and enthusiasm that arises from within as you act is what gives the joy.

People in whom the soul is awake simply do what they enjoy doing. They do it without wanting to achieve or become anything through that activity. Their sphere of influence may seem to be small or insignificant, but they leave it to the God to decide its value and significance.

When you understand this rule, you want to keep a kind and caring attitude; you want to do only what is just and proper; you refuse to act with an agitated mind; and you don't react negatively to other people's behaviour.

6. Do not lower yourself in the eyes of your conscience

It doesn't really matter if other people criticize you or call you foolish. Other people look upon you through a mind that is coloured by their personal motives, desires and fears.

However, it does matter if your actions lower you in the eyes of your own conscience. Whenever you feel lowered in the eyes of your conscience, know that you have not acted in God's way.

Insightful Notes:

The spiritual way is to consider what others have to say, but to make your own decisions by relying on God. Keep referring your affairs to God, and allow God to indicate what you must do to keep dharma (or truth) on your side.

Then follow the indications you have to the best of your ability. That is sufficient. Leave the rest to God.

Your conscience has a higher level intelligence than your intellect. So when your conscience shows you something clearly, you must accept it as true. If your conscience says "no", then leave it. Don't argue on it or attempt to go around it.

7. Your enemies are within you

The inner and outer aspects of your life are related. Your inner enemies are mirrored in the people you meet and in the difficulties you experience.

When you look upon your difficulties and enemies in this way, you don't blame others for your troubles. You look for the causes inside your nature and try to eliminate them there. When you have done that, the difficulties and obstacles also disappear from your outer life!

Insightful Notes:

Always look upon your difficulties as tests that are given to you. Their purpose is to strengthen you and prepare you for greater challenges. You have to trust the higher consciousness and believe that you will not be tested beyond your capacity.

When you try to eliminate your troubles or enemies in outer life without removing their cause inside your nature, you never really succeed. The cause remains so the situations will recur in some form or another. The enemies or difficulties will continue to put you down.

Your behaviour in the outer world reflects what you are within. The world is the same for everyone, but how you perceive it makes it different. Some people find the heaven in it and other people find the hell in it. In management the saying is: *"Your glass is either half full or half empty. What you see depends on which side you see it from"*.

In the same way, the experience of beauty and wonder are not really in the outside world. You experience them from within you as responses to what you come across on the outside.

Once you understand the importance of the inner life, you know you have to correct the defects inside your nature. Then you do not blame others for your bad luck or troubles. You try to overcome the inner situation, and when you have done that sufficiently, the problem also disappears on the outside.

8. Do not impose your way on God

Who do you trust, your ego or God? When you are deserted, insulted, or frustrated and apparently God has not attended your call, do you discard your faith in God?

Know that God's power will not support you when you act according to your criteria or wishes. You cannot impose your way on God. Instead, you have to impose God's way in your mind. Follow the silent promptings you receive from God and things will automatically begin to auto-correct in your life.

Insightful Notes:

Whenever you try to use God's help to accomplish something that is mean or selfish, God simply withdraws. Then you are left to the limitations of your personal ability. The proper use of the higher consciousness is to use it to know the higher way. Then we have to follow the guidance we have received.

God's criteria cannot be understood with a mind that is obsessed with sensual desires or personal ambition. You should never try to have your criteria passed. Instead, you have to try to know what God wants you to do, and how God wants you to do it.

Your spiritual task is to keep your mind sufficiently open so that God can speak in it. Once you know the right thing to do, you have to overcome your inner resistance to doing it.

Do not waste your time and energy in pursuing egoistic pursuits. Such pursuits only take you farther away from God.

Everyone experiences times of stagnation – when you are unable to connect up with God. Then, you have to refresh your enthusiasm. To get started again read the sayings of sages, visit spiritual persons, and break the habit that has caused your alienation.

9. God always supports disinterested action

God's power acts quietly and without drawing attention to itself. Hence, when you act without personal considerations God's power is acting through you. When you act with personal motives God's power withdraws from you. Then, you are left to the limitations of your personal ability.

Hence, you have to be very careful when you act. Invite God to guide your actions. Seek to do only what God wants you to do; and do it as God wants you to do it. Seek only to serve God and become unconcerned about your personal success.

Insightful Notes:

The God consciousness includes everyone. Hence, God wants you to seek inclusive solutions. If you act with selfish or egoistic considerations, you degrade God's power in you.

You can only hold God's power when you act without selfish considerations. So try to serve a higher purpose or the larger interest, and become less concerned about your personal success! Allow your personal benefit to arise as only a desired side-effect of the benefit that you bring to others.

A Prayer

Dear God:
You are my Atma (my innermost spirit).
My nature is wedded to you.
This body is your dwelling.
With my vital forces I attend to you.
My longing for sensual pleasures I offer in your worship.
Even during sleep I contemplate on you.
All my wandering around in life is just going around you.
With words I express you.
Whatever actions I do, and their results also, I surrender to you my Lord.

Insightful Notes:

You can use this prayer to practice the presence of God. You can also use the mystical poems given under the title of '**Moments of Overflowing**' for this purpose. In addition to these prayers, use the assurance given below to arouse spiritual feelings and increase your trust in God.

An Assurance:

Imagine that your Deity is looking at you and saying to you as follows:

I am with you, and I will always be with you until the end of the world.

Drop all your fears and insecurities at my feet, and work quietly in my assurance, and without seeking selfishly.

Whenever you are confronted with terrifying circumstances, don't be afraid.

Remember, I know all this, and I am with you.

Give up all your dependence on people, circumstances, and the conditions of the world; and rest only in me.

© 2011-2018, Prashant S. Shah

I know your needs, and it is my pleasure to provide for you, and not to make you struggle and strive.

Always listen to my quiet voice, and know that I will never forsake you.

A Conversation

Student: How can I get a qualification in mysticism?

Master: It is a practice and not a study, and it won't get you a paid job.

Student: What if I still I want to pursue it?

Master: Then you must prepare yourself.

Student: What do I have to do?

Master: Lower yourself.

Student: That is simple; here I bow.

Master: You have to learn to stay down. Many forces will arise from within you to resist this decision. And you have to overcome them to gain in strength.

Insightful Notes:

Here is an interesting passage in the praise of humbleness. It is from Tao Te' Ching, Passage-22 (my version):

The Sages hold on to the Tao through humbleness and model their lives by attuning with it.
Just because they do not see themselves (their own wishes), they see clearly.
Just because they do not assert themselves, their decisions find acceptance.
Just because they do not boast, they their actions can show their merit.
Just because they do not become proud, their accomplishments are long lasting.
Just because the Sages do not contend for themselves, no one quarrels with them!

The ego or the mental-self can be dislodged in two ways. One way is to regard the soul as your connections with the Lord and to proactively try and serve the Lord. The other way is to lower the ego by adopting the attitude of humility.

Humility does not replace the ego, but it makes the ego harmless and manageable. However, since the ego is not eradicated it can return in you weak moments. Then it can ruin the progress you have made over the years.

The ego is truly overcome when you replace it with the God consciousness. When God becomes the doer in your life, the ego takes on an object-like existence. In this condition the ego can be used to carry out some tasks, but it cannot assert itself or decide for you.

Conversation continued:

Student: How can I live for something greater than myself?

Master: Serve God.

Student: Which organisation should I join to serve God?

Master: You want a paid or unpaid job in an organisation?

Student: I mean I can serve in an organisation that serves God.

Master: Then you serve the organisation, and you may not serve God.

Student: Okay, how can I directly serve God?

Master: You can do that by doing what you see as necessary, but without showing yourself.

© 2011-2018, Prashant S. Shah

Insightful Notes:

People have come to regard many things as spiritual. They think that 'a religious topic, 'a place of worship', 'a person wearing a religious robe', or 'an office bearer of a religious institution' are all spiritual. Such things or persons sometimes carry a spiritual influence, but these days that is usually not the case.

In the modern times falsehood has been mixed with truth, and spirituality has been falsified. It has been taken up and managed by people who are themselves inadequate for the subject. Hence, there is a lot of deception. You cannot take anything at their 'face value'. Even many things that are apparently true are being used to promote falsehood. So, you have to be watchful.

Conclusion:

The practice of mysticism will transform your motives and point of view. It will develop your insight and awareness, and ultimately lead you to God experience. Here you find lasting peace and contentment, which cannot be got through people and things of the world.

© 2011-2018, Prashant S. Shah

Insightful Notes:

Once you accept the way of mysticism, you have to pursue it sincerely. Make all your decisions consciously by referring them to God. God will give you the indications. If the indication in some matter says: *"No"*; you will know it. Then you must leave it and look for something else.

Whenever you do things with ulterior motives, sooner or later you fall into a trap. However, when you know you are in a trap, refuse to stay trapped. In business they would say: *"Cut your losses and get out without losing all your investments."*

When you follow God's way, you keep God and truth on your side. Just hold on to them and you will go all the way.

MOMENTS OF OVERFLOWING

These poems depict deep feelings that arise at the different stages on the mystical path. They express clearly, in just a few words, what cannot be conveyed through extensive descriptions. You can contemplate on these verses to feel the divine presence.

The Poems:
1. The Call
2. Patient Waiting
3. The Ego
4. Your Cupbearer
5. You Lead And I Follow
6. You Are My Strength
7. I Live For You
8. The Awakening

© 2011-2018, Prashant S. Shah

1. The Call

**The pride in me would say,
"I do not beg, nor do I pray."
But one day a call quietly came in to say,
"Hold my hand and I'll show you the way."
I held the hand, just to know.
But now, I never want to let go.**

Insightful Notes:

When an egg is hatched, it cracks open. In the same way, when you arrive at a critical stage in your journey on earth, you find some reason to embark on a spiritual path. It may be some dissatisfaction; you may want to find a love that lasts; you could be intrigued by the mysterious or the miraculous; or you may simply want to make your life more valuable by living for a cause that is greater than yourself.

Whatever it is, first you get a call from within. Next, you find some excuse to look to what it shows. Ultimately your heart takes over and you go for it; you feel committed to go wherever it may lead you.

2. Patient Waiting

Would you pluck a flower before it has blossomed?
Would you crush a sprouting seed?
Through patient waiting they ripen.
So also our unexpressed thoughts and unfinished works
Must await their time for harvesting.

Insightful Notes:

Everyone wants to progress quickly. So, when your progress is slow (or not at all) you become very impatient.

But everything in nature has to pass through the necessary stages before it matures. A baby doesn't start running. First, it learns to turn over. Next, it begins to crawl. Then, it learns to stand up and balance. And later on it manages to take a few steps forward.

In the same way, you also have to pass through the stages. Each stage serves to prepare you for what is to come next. So, they test your readiness for taking up what is ahead.

What happens when you try to arrive before you are ready? Then the opportunity hasn't arrived for you. So you get frustrated thinking you have come to the wrong place; or the opportunity just passes by, and you are unable to hold on to it or make something of it.

3. The Ego

**You were the first occupant of my house.
So, as a friend, I trusted you.
But you and your companions are no friends of mine.
You bring in only trouble and strife.
Henceforth, stay away from this house;
For now, this is my masters' dwelling.**

Insightful Notes:

In the early stages of your practice your actions are motivated by the ego. You cannot begin to pursue something unless your ego is tempted. And you cannot continue to pursue it unless the ego permits. Otherwise you sulk, become impatient, or threaten to give up the pursuit.

However, as you progress on the path you can see how the ego is setting up or causing the troubles in your life. It changes your attitude towards the ego. You don't want to do things for ego satisfaction. Instead, you look for ways that can get you out of clutches of the ego!

4. Your Cupbearer

You keep filling my cup.
But I spill it again and again.
I've so often scattered your gift,
But you still fill it again.
Truly, I do not know how to fill this cup.
I only know that you have placed this cup in my hand.
You give and you keep;
I am only your humble cupbearer.

Insightful Notes:

As your insight matures, you understand that the talent you have and the opportunities you get in life are not really deserved. They are granted to you. Hence, you feel grateful to have them.

Then, your achievements do not make you proud; you do not claim greatness; and you know that you are worth very little without God's support. Then you are happy to just do what needs to be done and go unnoticed.

5. You Lead and I Follow

I look back upon the mess I have made and ask:
"Could it have been better?"
But you say: "Whatever happened had to happen."
So now I have stopped striving for myself
And only seek to serve you.
Now you lead and I follow.
And everything turns out just right.

Insightful Notes:

When your guiding intelligence is the mind, you are blindly led by your desires and tendencies. They decide for you. It makes you assert your rights and push your claims. But when you act in this way you don't feel good about it.

However, once a higher principle has awakened in you, something strange happens. The resistance in your mind disappears. The in the outer world also you don't have to assert your agenda or force anything to happen. You only quietly serve the truth.

But does that make you incapable or ineffective? On the contrary, you work peacefully, you feel happy to do the work, and the work or result turns out much better.

6. You Are My Strength

As light dispels darkness,
You have overcome my formidable foe.
What I tried so hard to do, but could not,
You have done in just one stroke.
Now that you have come, I feel safe.
Please stay with me.
I have no strength without you.

Insightful Notes:

Some of your tendencies are deeply entrenched in the subconscious. Hence, you don't know how they arise or what empowers them. So, you helplessly give in to them; and in turn they make you dance to their tune.

However, when you can access a higher power and allow it to guide you and act through you, everything changes. The higher power begins to accomplish through you. Then, what you could not do by yourself, it does for you.

7. I Live For You

I first came to you with a load of things.
So I could not take your gift.
I tried to pick something from here and there,
But you would not let me make my mix.
So disappointed, I returned to shed the load.
Now I come empty and unaccompanied,
To take whatever you may give, and do your wish.
Mine is gone, and yet I remain.
I have emptied, and yet I'm filled.
Now I live, but it is for you.

Insightful Notes:

God is for everyone. Hence, you cannot use God's power to serve your egoistic or selfish purposes. It would be a misuse. However, you can use God's power to overcome your ego.

People say that God is with us and so success will be ours. But God seems to ask: *"Are you really with me?" "Do you want success for yourself or do you want to accomplish something for me?"*

To live spiritually is to live for God; to follow God's way; to serve God; to depend on God; and to let God to look after you.

8. The Awakening

**The sound of your mantra has aroused me –
Who was lost in idle dreams.
I woke up just for a moment,
But something has turned over inside me.
Now, even in sleep
Something is still awake and watching.
That which you have awakened sleeps no more.**

Insightful Notes:

When your awareness is at the surface, your mind is restless and constantly chattering. However, when your awareness goes deeper, you experience calm, and you can perceive everything clearly.

When your awareness goes deep your awareness shifts onto a higher consciousness. This consciousness is not body based. Hence, it does not sleep when the mind and body sleep. It is always awake, and it watches over you. It can inform you, guide you, warn you, and also accomplish things for you.

A Journey into the Higher Worlds

A Pilgrimage into the Cosmos Within

We are born with a mind that directs our attention outward, towards things in the external world. Hence, we do not see the interior world or understand the realities of inner life. As a result we are easily confused about the true purpose of our life on earth or what we have come here to achieve.

To understand such things in the spiritual context, we have to journey into our interior; into the deeper realms of our own consciousness. *What do we find?* Here are some insights of this journey.

© 2011-2018, Prashant S. Shah

1. Our condition at the beginning

In the beginning, that is before we undertake the journey within, into the interior of our own consciousness, our attention is exclusively turned outward, towards things in the external world. To begin this journey we have to withdraw some of our attention from outer things and direct it inward, into our interior.

At first this will be very difficult to do. Our mind is like a restless monkey. It keeps on hopping from one thing to another. It keeps us continuously distracts by outer things. We get fascinated by them. However, we cannot dwell on any one thing for sufficient time to really understand it. So, we observe everything superficially, and our understanding remains shallow.

Our attention it totally caught up with personal thoughts. So we keep on think of ourselves, our pending matters, our desires, our possessions, or our future.

2. Taking control of our attention

We can change this wandering tendency of the mind by practising concentration. Earlier our mind was like a 'wild horse', constantly resisting our control and distracting our attention. But as our concentration improves, this wild horse gets tamed. Our mind begins to listen to us; our attention follows our will.

We can use concentration practice to bring together all the scattered forces of our attention. When these different forces come together they are compelled to adjust and integrate themselves under the central leadership of our will. It makes our will strong and powerful.

We can use this strong will-power to control the thoughts and emotions that frequently occupy our mind. We do it by simply accepting the thoughts and emotions that we want, and by rejecting those we don't want. In this way we can remove the distracting thoughts and disturbing emotions from our mind. It will make our mind becomes calm, alert and one-pointed.

Such a mind allows us to observe its contents – the thoughts and emotions that occupy it; and the mindset – the beliefs and tendencies that we use to interpret the happenings of life. We see how our habits and tendencies compel our behaviour. We see how these forces dominate our thinking and feelings, and decide our beliefs.

Now we can begin to change this inner situation; to free our mind from the compulsions created by our habits and tendencies. However, when we try to change or re-set our habits and tendencies is that we only succeed in making some superficial or cosmetic changes; and even these changes are not long lasting. That is, when we relax our control the habits and tendencies tend to return.

That happens because our habits and tendencies are rooted in the subconscious, whereas our will-power is mainly functional in the conscious mind.

3. The nature of the subconscious

The subconscious is a dark region of our mind. It is called 'dark' because here we do not see things clearly. Hence, we cannot observe how the forces work in this region.

We see things clearly at the surface, in the conscious mind; but here also our control is limited. That happens because some of these forces are supplied from below, from the subconscious.

So, what happens when we try to uproot a small or insignificant habit or tendency? The habit tends to return. That happens since the habit is empowered by the thoughts, emotions and desires that are connected with it in the subconscious. Since we do not see these connections clearly we take a compromising approach and settle for some small adjustments.

4. What we see in the subconscious

However, we can learn to take the 'light of our awareness' into the subconscious and observe these forces. Then we see the 'hidden contents' of our mind – our suppressed desires and emotions. They live here, and every now and then they come into our conscious mind and make us indulge them. Further, they make us justify having them. It gives them a hold in our nature and the right to return. In this way they break our will to resist them.

When we can see the working of these forces clearly, we know that our tendencies have friends. They have made connections, associations and alliances with other forces in the subconscious. So, when we try to overcome even a simple habit, we are not we are not dealing with just one thing, but we are dealing with a whole web of forces. This web of forces is strong, and it can resist our effort to change. So what seems to be simple actually turns out to be difficult and complex.

The habits and tendencies of our nature are like 'entities' that have a parasite-like existence. They feed on our attention by keeping a hold over our vital urges, inclinations, imagination and mindset. However, once we see all this clearly we can begin to uproot our tendencies and change our habits.

5. The inner battle

Before we change or uproot any habit or tendency, first we have to weaken it. We do it by finding its connections in our mind and disconnecting them.

For example, if we want to overcome our craving for some food, we must begin by developing an aversion to having it. It will reduce its power.

Initially the tendency is strong like a lion, but after we cut its connections it becomes weak like mouse. We cannot throw out the lion, but we can easily close up the mouse hole.

Once the tendency has lost its power, it cannot move us with its suggestions; it cannot decide our behaviour; and it cannot make us dance to its tune.

However, these entities don't leave us without putting up a fight. They may try to seduce us into believing that a life without (indulging) them will be dull, dry and uninteresting. And if we are taken up by such suggestions, we give them the right to continue or persist. Then they can again become active and try to dominate our awareness.

It is expected that there will be many battles inside the mind, and so for some time we may struggle. But if we persist, we will succeed. And the behaviour, urges, beliefs and philosophy that were built around this habit or tendency will also change.

© 2011-2018, Prashant S. Shah

6. After the victory

The entities in our subconscious do not have a power of their own; they merely draw it from our will-power. So, when we overcome some habit or tendency, our will-power gets stronger. And with a stronger will-power it will be easier for us to overcome other bigger or more vital habits and tendencies.

We can continue this process until we have overcome all the contradictory forces within our nature. It will overcome our inner resistance to doing anything. And as a result, our internal conflicts, aversions, and subconscious reactions to the happenings in the world will also disappear.

Earlier the forces in the subconscious would project illusions in our mind and tempt us or deceive us to scatter our force. But after we have cleared these entities from our subconscious, we do not experience wish or fear projections. Hence, we are not deceived easily. The light of our intellect pass right through the subconscious, so we see everything clearly. We do not act in ignorance and we are not easily fooled.

In the earlier stages of our spiritual practice we had to make a lot of effort to concentrate. Now our attention is free from the binding influences from the subconscious. Hence, no extra effort is needed. Our concentration is 'at will'. We simply focus on something and our attention gets concentrated around it.

7. The separate awareness

Then we can keep the habit of keeping our mind in a concentrated state. It develops a 'Separate Awareness' within our consciousness. Something separates from our personal nature, but remains within our consciousness. It is a calm, wide and alert state of mind. It sees everything clearly, but it remains unaffected by what it sees. We can use this separate awareness to develop our insight and have a multidimensional point of view.

Initially this 'separate awareness' remains in the background. So we have to concentrate upon it to access it. But gradually it develops into a faculty that we can use like other senses. It gives us clarity of vision and a sense of direction in life matters – it tells us where we should look for the truth. We still have to use the mind to work out the details, but with this faculty we don't have to depend on mental inferences.

8. The purpose of the separate awareness

The separate awareness greatly enlarges our field of knowledge and action. We can use it to look into the 'mind of things' and know the inner qualities and hidden motives in anything.

Further we can learn to transfer our will on to the separate awareness. It enables us to act on the inner planes of the cosmos and influence the happenings from there.

However, the true purpose of this faculty is not for making some things happen, but it is for integrating the forces within our own consciousness. It will change 'the state' of our consciousness and how we function with it.

9. Awareness beyond the mind

As we develop further, our awareness begins to recede inward. We become more conscious of our interior. First the contents of our mind (the thoughts, emotions, feelings and memories) become objective. Then the entire the interior worlds becomes objective, like external things.

Then we can awaken in our dreams and travel consciously in the interior worlds. We can make the light of our awareness bright and carry the greater light into the interior worlds. We become aware of so many things that earlier we could not even imagine.

At a certain stage in our development something turns over within our consciousness and we awaken inside the separate awareness. An inner veil is lifted, which enables us to become directly aware of things by making an inner contact. Then the automatic subconscious processes that were earlier going on in the mind also get discontinued.

Earlier we were led by social values and mental-inferences of right or wrong. Now we see such things as ignorant mental inferences that disturb the expression of living truth. Hence, we do not use them to function any more. We can draw our wisdom directly through direct awareness.

SPIRITUAL ALCHEMY

A subtle insight into the process of transforming the human nature

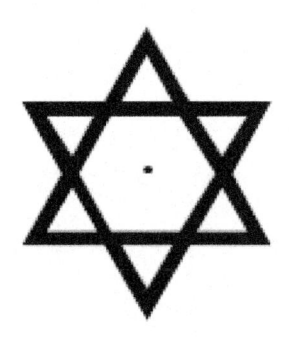

The Spiritual Balance of Soul and Nature

Alchemy is the process of transforming Lead, your ordinary nature, into Gold, a spiritual being. How is this process accomplished through Yoga? How does it unveil the mysteries of the cosmos?

Here we explain this process in terms of our growth in consciousness. It will also give an insight into esoteric doctrines like the Hermetic Wisdom and the Emerald Tablet.

© 2011-2018, Prashant S. Shah

1. The world as consciousness

Consciousness is the basic stuff and the creative essence of the universe. Movement of consciousness has created the universe and all that is in it. The same consciousness that manifests as the universe is also the Self, the spiritual essence, of every individual being that arises in it. Hence, the metaphysical structure of the world is like a 'woven fabric', wherein subject consciousness (the essence) is the vertical thread, and object consciousness (the substance) is the horizontal thread.

Since consciousness is everywhere, everything in the cosmos can be known. The consciousness in one form can connect with consciousness in another form and come to know things from inside out. This is direct knowing.

However, in human beings consciousness is identified with the mind and body. Due to this identification the power of pure consciousness (the Self) is reduced to a 'level of perception' in the human mind. The particular level of perception depends on what our consciousness is attached to or associated with, and on its conditioning in the individual. Hence, the human mind can only know things INDIRECTLY, through inference and interpretation. This semi-conscious and roundabout way of figuring things out is called 'mental knowledge'.

Alchemy speaks of purifying Lead and transforming it into Gold. In the spiritual context, it is the process of transforming the consciousness from being a narrow and inferring mental-consciousness, to becoming a wider and directly aware consciousness of the Self.

2. Our personal consciousness

When consciousness identifies with our body, we experience physical fears and sensual desires. When it identifies with the mind, we experience its tendencies, beliefs and conditioning. All these things put their limitations on our consciousness. They cloud the transparency of pure consciousness in our Nature. Hence, we do not experience the world with a pure consciousness, but we experience it with a personal consciousness.

The personal consciousness generates a duplicate-self, called the mental-self. This mental-self creates a personal world from our thoughts and emotions, and it keeps us constantly engaged with them. As a result we think in terms of 'me', 'my story', 'my likes', 'my fears', 'my desires', 'my way', and 'my possessions'.

3. The human situation

When we look deep into ourselves, into our subjective experience, instead of at the world, we can identify two parts of our being: One part is a consciousness that is totally calm. It sees and observes. We call it our Soul. The other part is a consciousness that is active and always doing something. It thinks and acts. We call it our Nature.

At the beginning of our spiritual quest these two parts of our being seem to be separate; they stand apart. The 'observer consciousness' is calm and reflective, whereas the 'doer consciousness' is restless and doing something.

We can understand the process of our growth in consciousness by relating these two parts of our being.

4. What is Bondage?

The Soul quietly observes the activity of our Nature and mirrors it in its own consciousness. The Nature or the doer consciousness, on the other hand, acts out of its own impulse, not caring about the will of the observer, the Soul. Hence, our Nature dominates, and the Soul has no say in the decisions and actions of our Nature.

Although these two parts of our being seem to be unrelated, there is a connection. The Soul observes the decisions and actions of our Nature, but it is unable to accept all of them. However, since the Soul is in a passive condition, it has to endure what it cannot accept. Hence, the association of Soul with our Nature is bondage for the Soul.

5. The Separation

On deeper observation we find that although our Nature can act out of its own impulse, to carry on in this way it needs the acceptance of the Soul. When the Soul was passive, Nature took this acceptance automatically. However, once the Soul is awake, it can refuse to grant its acceptance.

When our Nature acts according to the wishes of the Soul, the Soul accepts all the actions of our Nature. It does this by mirroring these actions in its consciousness. However, when Nature acts against the wishes of the Soul, the Soul can withhold its acceptance. It does this by refusing to mirror the actions of our Nature.

The Soul is an independent consciousness that lives in the spiritual world. When we identify ourselves with the Soul, we can separate ourselves from our Nature. Then the contents (thoughts, desires and emotions) of our mind become like objects. We can look upon them as things within us, but separate from us; we can remain unaffected by them. When we exercise this option, we are liberated from our bondage to a purely mental existence. We have a mind and body, but we experience ourselves as separate from them.

6. What is Purification?

The Soul is an independent consciousness, whereas our Nature is a derived consciousness; it is formed in nature, but derived from impressions carried by the soul. Hence, our Nature arises out of the Soul and depends on it for its sustenance. The Soul has power over Nature and it can exercise the power.

The Soul sees the actions of our Nature and quietly mirrors them in its consciousness. By mirroring them it sanctions them. However, when our Nature acts out of its own impulse, the Soul can also refuse to mirror its actions. Then our Nature has to change its ways. Thus, the seeing of the Soul acts as a command for our Nature.

To experience the Soul consciousness we have to find something within us that is independent of the continuously changing thoughts and forms of life. Once we find this consciousness, we have to identify with it. Then we can know the right movement; we can know what the Soul wants our Nature to do. Then further, through a process of approving or disapproving the actions of our Nature, we can purify it and make it transparent to the Soul.

7. The Alchemical Marriage

Alchemy uses the alternate movements of 'separation' and 'purification' to know and change the habits, tendencies and conditioning of our

Nature. As our Nature gets purified we overcome the contradictory energies and divisions within our consciousness. Then the Soul and our Nature begin to dance to one tune. Our Nature acts according to the wishes of the Soul; and the Soul accepts all the actions performed by our Nature. This is the famous alchemical marriage or 'MATING' in consciousness.

From this mating a new consciousness is born, which is undivided and totally different from our earlier 'mental consciousness'. It is neither subjective nor objective, but something all inclusive and beyond. This consciousness holds the key to the mysteries of the cosmos.

THE COMING OF THE NEW ERA

There is a spiritual presence that stands behind the activity of our mind. It oversees our actions and understands us deeply. It also oversees the actions of people and the happenings in the world.

Although the nature of this spiritual presence is a mystery for us, we can learn to relate with it and bring it forward in our life. That is the spiritual purpose of our life.

Thus true purpose of our life is not concerned with improving our living standards or increasing our power in society. Such things can only have a passing value. It is concerned with the kind of person we are becoming and the extent to which we are able to involve the spiritual presence in our life.

Here we call the 'spiritual presence' a higher-level consciousness. We contrast it with our ordinary (mental) consciousness and show what happens when the higher consciousness begins to awaken in our inner life.

We also address the issue of finding our purpose in life and the conditions under which we have to do it.

The two levels of our consciousness

There is *mortal part* of us, the mental-self, which is running our outer life today. It is selfish and self-centred, and we all know it. However, there is also an *immortal part* of us, a soul, which gives us our sense of conscience and the feeling of unity. These two parts are like two beings within us. Both of them are represented in our mind, but individually they function at two *separate levels* of consciousness.

We can understand the two levels of our consciousness by COMPARING our life to the life of a tree: A tree has a trunk and leaves. The leaves come and go according to the seasons, but the trunk sustains for longer. Further, the consciousness in the leaf is essentially the same as the consciousness in the trunk. However, when the consciousness *is confined to a part*, the powers of consciousness are contracted. Then the consciousness in the part experiences itself as an individual with interests that are separate from the whole. Thus, the leaf experiences the burning in summer, the chill in winter, and the fear of extinction in the fall season; but the trunk does not experience this fear. It grows over the years.

In the same way, our perception and insight into life *depend on how we regard and consider ourselves*. If we consider ourselves to be just a body with a mind, we experience ourselves as separate individuals with selfish interests. The consciousness in us gets confined to our mind and body. And we live mainly to satisfy the desires in our mind and body. Thus we think in terms of comforts, sensual thrills, money and prestige.

However, when we consider our identity as a soul, the in-dweller, we regard our mind and body as our possessions, like our car or house. Then our consciousness expands, and we can experience spiritual qualities and the higher values of life; we regard the forms of life and the conditions we are passing through as something temporary, like the leaves that come and go.

Further, the focus of our life shifts from outer growth to inner growth. Just as the trunk of a tree grows as it passes through the seasons, our inner life also matures as we assimilate our varied experiences from our existence on earth. Thus, the experiences of our mortal life mature the seeds of our immortal life. What we develop within us, stays with us; and we experience it as the STATE of our consciousness.

The Process of Spiritual Growth

Both the ordinary and the higher level consciousness are always reflected in our mind. However, initially we function mainly at the ordinary level. That is, we serve the mental-self, and in turn it keeps us preoccupied with physical activity and egoistic pursuits.

Our soul also has its influence in our mind. However, we give it so little attention that it seems to be something vague, hesitant and far removed. The result is that we do not experience the 'unity principle'; our 'truth sense' is weak; and we cannot perceive any 'deeper purpose' to our life.

Higher Nature/Divine Portion = **Soul**

↗ ↕

The Mind of Man _ _ _ _ _ _ ↕ line *of progress* →

↘ ↕

Lower Nature/Animal Portion = **Mental-Self**

To grow spiritually, we REVERSE this situation. We can do that by simply changing our 'point of view'.

Instead of looking upon everything from the ordinary level, and giving an ordinary meaning to higher things, we have to begin to look upon everything from the higher level, and try to give a spiritual significance to higher things. When we can do that sufficiently, it will change the 'level' of our perceptions. It will change 'from where' we see and 'from what depth' we see.

Gradually we can see everything as a part of a much LARGER PICTURE: Then we can situate everything correctly; we can put each thing into its proper place; we can look at the significance of what is happening; and we can also know the motives that are involved. As a result we are not easily deceived by outer appearances.

The Spiritual Purpose of our life

When we function mainly with the ordinary consciousness, we only hear the voice of our mental-self. It says: *"Play it safe and do as others are doing. Don't try to be insightful or take unnecessary risks — you may have to face unnecessary difficulties, rejection or failure."* But when we follow the ordinary consciousness we live as a pretender or worse, as a commuter — someone who has to get up every morning with the crowd and do the job just to earn enough money to pay the bills. We may live comfortably, be able to pay our bills on time, and do everything by the book. But after doing all this we still feel that such a life is not really worth living. We cannot feel enthusiastic about living in this way.

On the other hand, when we can mirror the higher consciousness in our mind we can sense the deeper purpose to our life. We feel happy to know that there is more to our life than being a commuter. We feel that there is a deeper purpose for which we have come to earth. Hence, we want to find it and serve it. And unless we do this we cannot be at peace with ourselves or feel fulfilled. So, we ask: *"What is the deeper purpose of my life? What is my mission? What is the work I have come to do?"*

Most people think of finding life's work in terms of career choices. However, it is more like involving the higher consciousness in the work we do. The task is to make our mind receptive to the higher consciousness and allow it to guide our actions and reorganise our inner-life. This task is complex and each one of us has to find our own answers, not intellectually, but by actually living our life. We do it in two parts. First we look for answers to our 'proximate issues'. And after we have done that we can ask questions relating to life issues.

When people begin their spiritual practice they often ask: *"What happens if my practice is not successful?"* Evidently they are looking for some tangible result –like mental or psychic power. However, if our task is to simply serve the higher consciousness, then the issue of achieving some tangible result becomes a non-issue. The effort itself becomes sacred; and the work itself becomes a privilege. Failure or success is only a mental judgement that we make against some expectation. In the true sense our failure is not pursuing what we have come here on earth to do!

The Coming of the New Era

In the book *'The Crisis of Modern Humanity'* we explained the concept of Cosmic Cycle and showed the significance of our times by describing the 'Signs of Our Times'. In particular, we showed the modern trend is to generate a false spirituality by making it rational or psychological. This trend is expected to continue until a 'critical point' is reached, when a radical change in orientation can be expected. This change would transform the conditions and purposes with which people live on earth. Something similar has also been declared by many visionaries over the past century. We return to this discussion because the critical point is near. Our purpose is not to scare our readers, but to prepare them for a smooth transition into the new era. We expect that 'fear based systems' of our times will be replaced in the next era by systems based on a higher-level consciousness.

To be able to participate in the making of the new era, we have to first cultivate spiritual qualities in our nature. We cannot allow fear, selfishness, greed or falsehood to motivate us. The extent of our difficulties will depend on the traits we have developed so far and how enthusiastic we are in making the necessary changes. The difficulties we may have to experience will not be caused by the new era; they will arise due to our attachment to the modern life-style, which is a product of the ordinary-level consciousness.

Today all kinds of practices have sprung up under the banner of 'New Age Practices'. To name a few, you have past-life regression therapy, psychoanalysis, tantric worship, scientology, pyramid therapy, ceremonial magic and elaborate ritual practices. Many shops have arisen to sell 'New Age Products' and numerous 'New Age Gurus' have come in to market their 'brand' of spirituality. The symbols and techniques that were used to prepare a person for spiritual living have been hijacked today. People now use them with the opposite intent – to pursue their egoistic and mundane goals. The title of 'New Age' has also become a brand for generating business opportunities!

Much of the 'New Age Information' is propagated through the internet. It is cleverly adapted to promote commercial interests and gain cheap popularity. People sometimes ask: *"Why true spirituality cannot become popular with the masses?"* The answer is simple. Popularity requires a wide base; and the masses, particularly in our modern times, are most uncomprehending. Hence, if something has to be made popular, it has also to be **brought down** to the level of comprehension of the masses. On the other hand spirituality seeks to

lift up the person, so that he or she can become adequate for higher knowledge. But lifting the level of our comprehension is something each one of us has to do for ourselves. It is not something that someone else can do for us. Hence, it is expected that true spirituality will remain unpopular with the masses.

People who live by selfishness, greed, sensuality, corruption and falsehood will certainly find it difficult to function in the new era. Their personal value system will collapse and they may find it difficult to adjust to the new higher-value system. Hence, they may fall out.

However, there are many persons who accept the terms of the new era. They want to participate in the change that is happening without getting disoriented. Here we address them here.

When the critical point is reached, each one of us has to make a DECISIVE CHOICE. Either we go along with the spirit of the New Era (by overcoming our preoccupation with our lower nature and our attachments to the ordinary life) or we continue to live according to the norms of the ordinary life. If we choose the former, we can catch the truth in life and get lifted. If we ignore this choice, we can fall out or face rejection.

How can I Participate?

Many spiritual seekers have asked this question in one way or another. What they really want to know is how they can actively participate in preparing for the new era. Here we indicate the way.

The ordinary-level consciousness dominates the modern world today. However, it may become dysfunctional in the new era. When a person works with the ordinary level consciousness without any higher influence, he or she becomes selfish and cunning. The ordinary consciousness dehumanises the social life; mechanises the work; and generates monstrous growths in society in the form of insanity, cruelty, corruption, and vulgar entertainment.

These monsters do not arise from the ordinary-level consciousness; they arise from the sub-human levels after the human being has been cut off from the higher-level influence. Without the spiritual influence of the higher consciousness a person can be easily swayed by sub-human influences that arise from the nether worlds.

Many strange and new things are arising in the modern world in the name of liberal and democratic values. They are not unexpected. They only show the decay in spirit, the decay in thought, and the decay in public life — at least from the spiritual or traditional point-of-view.

Each person has to reverse this trend within themselves. Then they can extend 'their presence' to the society they are involved with.

The KEY idea of Spirituality is that wisdom and the higher values of life arise naturally in the mind when we make it responsive to a higher or spiritual consciousness. Thus, wisdom is never the result of developing the ordinary consciousness, which is what is wrongly attempted through modern education! Wisdom is the result of disciplining the mind and making it responsive to the higher consciousness.

No amount of supervision or legislature can curb personal and social evils. It can only be brought about by involving the higher consciousness in the individual and in public life. We can do it by serving the higher consciousness; and it won't happen when we remain indifferent to it.

The higher consciousness lifts our thinking, our values, and our inner worth. It will reorganise our nature, and make us responsive to higher things. Then we can use our presence to re-organise the social systems we are involved with. In this way we can participate in establishing the higher consciousness in humanity.

On Promoting a Spiritual Mission

The primary aim of any mission is to spread its message so that it can REACH the people who are capable of using it. The secondary aim is to provide a 'support services' to those who want to IMPLEMENT the message in their life.

However, for a mission to remain genuine, it has to also employ means that are in harmony with its aim. And that raises the question of motivation: *"Should the mission be run like a 'business for profit' or as a non-profit (not non-profitable) service organisation?"*

What is the difference? When a business is focuses on generating profits, it attract profiteers and people who side-track the organisation onto selling. A non-profit service organisation, on the other hand, can focus on providing genuine value without indulging in seductive claims and deceptions just to improve their numbers. Such an organisation will lack the means (money) to carry out its mission, but it should not change its ways just to get more money.

What are the implications? You invite people who really want to 'serve the cause' and not encourage people who come in with the ulterior aim of using the opportunity to grow their personal business. The people have to be attracted with qualitative benefits and not with quantitative (financial) rewards. If they lack the motivation, it is better that they don't join.

A Review Request

Now that you have read the book so far, could you grant me the favour of writing a review on Amazon?

It will do two things: It will tell other readers what they can realistically expect from reading this book; and it will tell me what you want or value so that I can, in future, produce the kind of books that will benefit my readers the most. *Here are the steps:*

- Click Amazon.com or the Amazon site in your country.
- Sign into Amazon as you are prompted.
- Select an appropriate rating.
- Write a few honest words that describe your impressions in a box.
- Give a heading to the box.
- Click the 'submit' button

It's easy to do and I'll really appreciate it.

Click http://www.amazon.com/dp/B00AXI9BRW/

Thanks.
Prashant

© 2011-2018, Prashant S. Shah

Appendix

About the Author

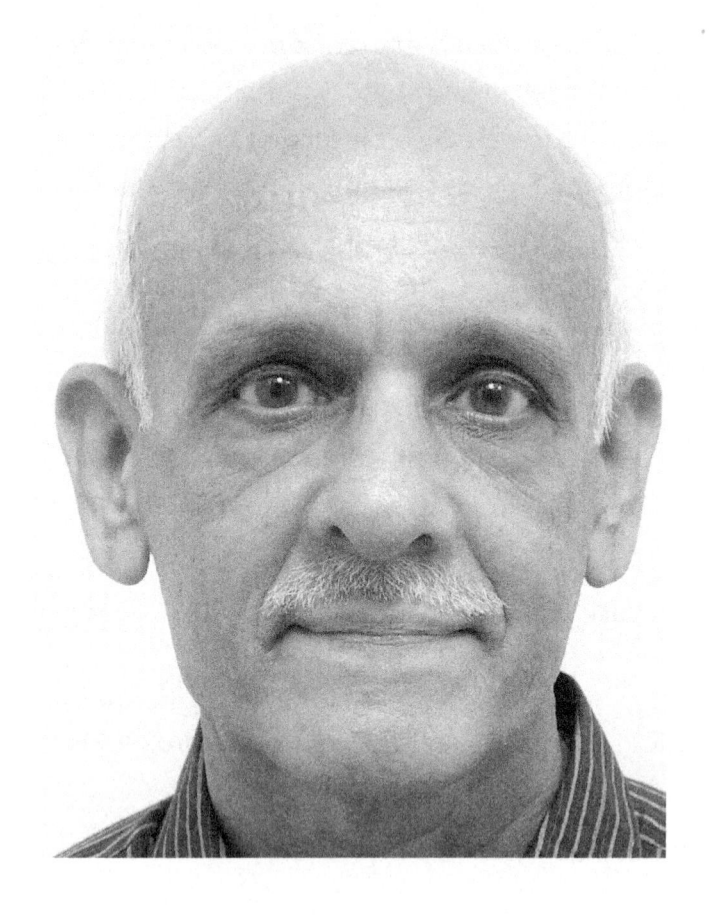

© 2011-2018, Prashant S. Shah

He was educated in science from Massachusetts Institute of Technology (MIT, USA) and University of California at Santa Cruz (UCSC, USA). During his student days he learnt Mysticism from Shri Nyaya Sharma, a Master of Shiva Tantra Yoga. He offers Spiritual Guidance through Darshana Centre, a School of Yoga-Mysticism at Baroda, India. He learnt Homoeopathy from Post Graduate Homoeopathic Association, Bombay, has healing hands and uses Pranic Healing. He learnt entrepreneurial skills through EKS, an Advanced Management Diploma Program offered by 'Mewes Systems' of Frankfurt, Germany. He uses EKS and Vedic Astrology for Counselling.

He has been conducting 'spiritual awareness workshops' regularly in USA, and from time to time in India. He is the Author of many self-help and spiritual books and Speaker on related subjects. He speaks clearly, in simple language and from personal experience.

His books are as follows: *Crisis of Modern Humanity (1976), The Essence of Hindu Astrology* — see them on his site under Books; his more recent publications are *The Art of Awakening the Soul*

© 2011-2018, Prashant S. Shah

(2011), *Healing without Drugs* (2014), *Solving the Problems of Life* (2015), *The Biochemic Prescriber* (2016) and *Restore your Health Naturally* (2017-18). These books are available from the Amazon and Kindle online bookstores.

For information on the books, articles and workshops by the author, visit the site on Internet at http://spiritual-living.in

© 2011-2018, Prashant S. Shah

About Darshana Centre

A School of Yoga-Mysticism

E-mail: darshanacentre@gmail.com

Darshana Centre has been conducting spiritual courses through correspondence since 1988. The courses are practical, practise based, and without religious bias. They are designed to help you in implementing the mystic philosophy.

There are four courses:

Course-1: Mind Training & Meditation

You learn to concentrate your mind and get control over your attention. Then you use it to clear up negative thoughts and emotions from your mind. This is important since your happiness and well-being depends more on how you handle your thoughts and emotions, and less on your external circumstances.

The practice of concentration will make your mind alert, calm, and cooperative. Then you will think clearly, understand better, and become more capable in whatever you undertake to do.

© 2011-2018, Prashant S. Shah

Course-2: Mantra Yoga

Here you learn to meditate with a mantra. Then you use it to organise your inner life. The mantra technique is a unique heritage that is passed down by tradition through a line of Masters.

Any mantra can be used as a seed for doing concentration practice, but when you want to use it to get on the spiritual path you should take the mantra from someone in whom it is awake. You can always light a fire by rubbing stones, but it is much easier to light a fire with fire.

Mantra Yoga is a complete practice by itself. Once the mantra has settled in you, a spiritual presence will arise in your mind. It will assist you and guide you at every stage on the spiritual path.

Course-3: Yoga-Mysticism

Just as behind the superficial existence of a leaf there is a greater existence of the tree, so also behind our individual and personal consciousness there is the 'greater consciousness' of the soul and the over-soul.

In this course you learn to install a presence of the greater consciousness in your mind and begin to involve it in your affairs. Then, instead of being led astray by egoistic tendencies and desires in your mind and body, you will be guided by the prompting of a higher consciousness.

Course-4: Advanced Spiritual Practice

The spiritual pursuit is not about worshipping Gods, performing rituals or following some moral precepts. The main aim is to clear the impurities from your mind so that you can clearly mirror the calm, intelligent and balanced state of the higher consciousness.

In accomplishing this task, the objective techniques like concentration, prayer, meditation and yoga-asana can only help you to an extent. To have a breakthrough you have to overcome the forces within your nature that resist the higher consciousness! This work is more about unlearning and correcting the faults in your mindset; and less about learning new things.

In this course first you understand the psychological processes that are behind spiritual growth. Next, you observe the mental tendencies that obstruct your spiritual awareness. Then, you try to overcome these tendencies and clear the faults in your perceptions. As you do that you begin to see yourself, others and situations of life not as they show themselves, but as they really are.

For Details on these Courses, click here: https://darshanacentre.wordpress.com/2015/12/30/courses-for-spiritual-awakening/

Advantages of learning through Correspondence

Some people wonder how someone can learn to do spiritual practice through a correspondence course. Hence, it calls for some explanation.

You do not grow spiritually by learning some philosophy or by following a belief system. You grow by doing your spiritual practice under the supervision of a Guru.

Our basic instruction is given through lessons. You study a lesson and do the practise for a period of time. Then, you answer the questions of the lesson and email it to us. The issues usually become clearer to you when you make out your answers AFTER doing the practise. On our part, we read your answers and give you appropriate feedback. Then, we give you the next lesson. We maintain your file and monitor your progress.

© 2011-2018, Prashant S. Shah

These courses are practical. Hence, you are only given the information you need to do the practices properly. As you do the practices you will actually develop the skills and capacities that are necessary to build your inner life. We ensure that you do not skip the necessary steps, for the spiritual practice is a sure process only when it is taken as a whole.

We administer information to you in a stepwise manner so that you can accomplish difficult things by taking small and convenient steps. You can also have your personal difficulties solved as you go along. Further, you can learn at your pace, in the convenience of your home, and practice in your environment. In addition, we have a provision for a personal meeting with our students. You can visit us or meet through the internet.

An Invitation

Dear Reader,

After carefully reading the BROCHURE, think it over. Do you feel there is some deep mystery underlying your existence, and that unless you uncover this mystery you cannot be satisfied, and your life will be without any deep meaning? Are you willing to give up some superficial things in your outer life so that some deeper satisfaction can arise from within you?

© 2011-2018, Prashant S. Shah

Will you be able to devote a half-hour every morning and evening for your spiritual practice?

If you are thinking of taking these Courses mainly because you wish to develop some 'psychic powers' (something that will give you importance or an unfair advantage over others), please DON'T. The true spiritual powers won't arise in any measure before you have changed your motives and point of view. Your object in taking these Courses should not be to 'have more' externally, but to 'be more' internally.

However, if you sincerely want to grow spiritually, then here is an opportunity that you should not miss. You will have the guidance that you need. You will use methods that have worked under the conditions of the modern world. Please don't entertain unnecessary doubt, suspicion or fear regarding spiritual development. Here you do not lose; you only get rid of the unwanted. If you have been doing spiritual practice, but you still feel the need for personal guidance, then also these Courses are for you.

Prashant

The Message

You may have read several books, taken spiritual courses, and practised some meditation techniques on your own for years without making any significant progress. However, take a set of personalised lessons from an expert and your practice will suddenly leap ahead.

BOOKS

1. Healing Without Drugs

A Simple Solution to your Health Problems
Contains the Essence of Naturopathy, Water Therapy and Pranic Healing

© 2011-2018, Prashant S. Shah

166 pages; ISBN-13: 978-145242793; ISBN-10: 149524279X; ASIN: B00HYR3RRA. The URL is http://www.amazon.com/dp/B00HYR3RRA

The Message:

Your health is always your concern and not your doctor's concern. However, today the people are made to believe that their health depends on doctors and the healthcare system! It has made the people unnecessarily dependent on the medical profession. On the other side the healthcare system has become extremely expensive, and the issues of health have become too technical and complicated for the common man to comprehend.

However, this should not dishearten you since you can learn to maintain your health with your own efforts. All you have to do is to think holistically and to take the simple self-help measures that can restore your health and keep you healthy. The know-how on how you can do it is adequately provided in this book.

The Methods:

Here you learn to use simple methods like good eating habits, elimination diets, water therapy, fasting, etc. to bring about lasting relief to many of your long standing problems. In this way you not only restore your health, but you also build your immunity to disease.

The book also talks about psychosomatic causes of diseases and how to deal with them. In particular, you learn to deal with the issues of stress, trauma, karmic causes, and how to benefit from pranic healing.

An Estimate:

Holistic healing is not something that is done to you. You have consciously or unconsciously participated in generating the causes of your ailment. Hence, you have to also participate in overcoming the cause. You have to make the necessary adjustments in your mindset, eating habits and emotions to overcome the cause of your ailments.

An Overview of the Chapters

- The 'Forward' and 'Preface' tell you the point of view adopted in this book.
- Chapter-1 discusses the basic concept of holistic healing.
- Chapter-2 explains the rationale of naturopathy.

- Chapter-3 discusses the most convenient and effective remedies for self-healing.
- Chapter-4 explores the deeper causes, like stress, trauma and karma, which underlie the basic disease factor of Toxaemia in the body.
- Chapter-5 discusses the theory and practice of pranic healing, which is exceptionally useful in healing deeper organ troubles, backaches, psychosomatic disorders and psychological troubles.

2. Solving the Problems of Life

For Spiritual Seekers

132 pages; ISBN-13: 9781518786655; ISBN-10: 1518786650; ASIN: B0176HQSOG. The URL is http://www.amazon.com/dp/B0176HQSOG

© 2011-2018, Prashant S. Shah

It is said that ships are safe in the harbour. But that is not what ships are made for. They are there so that we can sail through the rough seas and visit distant lands. In the same way we can suffer our problems and seek to avoid them; or we can treat them as opportunities to grow and enjoy the problem-solving process. *What will it be?*

When we think spiritually, we consider that the people who are involved with us and the happenings of our life are given to us. They provide us the opportunities that we need to grow. Just as a car needs the ground to move forward, a bird needs the air to fly, we need the resistance from life (the problems) to grow and mature.

This book will take you on a problem-solving journey. The journey passes through three chapters. First, you develop the right attitude towards your problems and life situation. Next, you go further and learn what you can do right now to experience freedom and contentment in your life. And lastly, you learn how to take control over your attention, and use it to overcome the problems created by your personal thoughts and emotions.

© 2011-2018, Prashant S. Shah

3. The Biochemic Prescriber

© 2011-2018, Prashant S. Shah

Biochemic medicine was discovered over a hundred years ago by a German physician, Dr. Wilhelm Heinrich Schuessler. He identified twelve inorganic tissue-salts that are essential for the healthy functioning of the human body. He showed that when there is a deficiency of any of these salts in the body tissues, certain typical symptoms arise. You can use these symptoms *to identify* the specific deficiency.

Then all you have to do is supplement the deficient tissue-salt in a dynamic (potency 6X) form. That will stimulate the vital force to become active and do the healing.

This system is simple to understand and easy to use. And it comes without the 'side-effects' that usually arise from using the drug therapy. The most interesting thing about this approach to healing is that you don't need to know in detail the functions of the body organs or the classification of disease; and you don't have to rely on all kinds of laboratory tests to be able to prescribe.

Here is an up-to-date, clear, and concise book that you can use to heal yourself, your family and friends. It tells you how you can treat the common

everyday ailments that arise. The book is simple to understand and easy to use; and the results are very consistent and satisfying. Available on Amazon and Kindle online bookstores:
https://www.amazon.com/dp/B01FA6X4FG/
http://www.amazon.com/dp/1533128065

The Contents

1. Some Reviews
2. Author's Preface
3. A Synopsis
4. Introduction
5. The Guiding Symptoms of the 12 tissue-salts
6. Tips for differentiating the remedies
7. Grouping of the tissue-salts
8. Tissue-salts in constitutional disorders
9. Treating inflammations
10. Treating an abscess
11. Treating pains
12. Treating headaches
13. Tissue-salts and body organs
14. Biochemic ointments
15. Tissue-salt indications from facial signs
16. The Prescription
17. Case taking

© 2011-2018, Prashant S. Shah

18. Repetitions
19. Do 'side-effects' arise from using these tissue salts?
20. Why are there no biochemic practitioners?
21. On Readymade Formulations
22. Leading Remedies for Common Diseases

4. How to Restore your Health Naturally

A time-tested way to heal yourself by simply changing your lifestyle and eating habits

ISBN-13: 978-1977555472; ISBN: 9781730738944; ISBN-10: 1977555470

© 2011-2018, Prashant S. Shah

Today we are ingrained to believe that our health depends on doctors, medicines, and the health care industry; whereas the truth is that our health really depends on our lifestyle, diet and emotions. When we understand this simple truth, we can learn to restore and maintain our health by our own efforts and, except in extreme cases, we will not need to consult doctors.

The method of natural healing shown here is holistic and totally different from the specialised advice that you normally receive from the medical profession. It is simple, and to use it you do not need to know anatomy, physiology, pathology, toxicology or pharmacology. Further, the results of this treatment are self-evident, and so you do not have to search for empirical proofs.

You simply learn to strengthen the vital force of the body and help it in its effort to restore your health or keep you healthy. This method works, not sometimes, but always.

Contents

1. Foreword
2. Introduction

© 2011-2018, Prashant S. Shah

3. The medical profession focuses on relieving symptoms
4. What is so wrong with just relieving symptoms?
5. The holistic and analytic approaches to healing
6. Understanding disease in terms of toxaemia and the vital force
7. Aren't germs and bacteria the causes of disease?
8. How to detoxify the body
9. Reduce the existing toxaemia
10. Avoid generating toxins
11. Correct your eating habits
12. On emotional causes
13. What causes the vital force to become weak?
14. The elimination crisis
15. If natural healing is so simple, why isn't everyone doing it?
16. Our message

Available from
https://www.amazon.in/dp/B075V5R1FJ

Printed in Great Britain
by Amazon